Activating the Light in the Lord's Prayer: the Infinite Course

Activating the Light in the Lord's Prayer: the Infinite Course

Margareth Lee

Writers Club Press
San Jose New York Lincoln Shanghai

Activating the Light in the Lord's Prayer: the Infinite Course

Writers Club Press
an imprint of iUniverse, Inc.

For information address:
iUniverse, Inc.
5220 S. 16th St., Suite 200
Lincoln, NE 68512
www.iuniverse.com

margarethlee@absolute1.net

ISBN: 0-595-24839-X

Printed in the United States of America

Contents

Foreword

In his book 'In Tune with the Infinite' (1915) Ralph Waldo Trine remarks, that 'the great world war...surely would not have been necessary, if we had lived our Christianity, instead of mainly lecturing about its Founder'. In this book that has been avoided. Here the teaching of the divinity of man, so concisely framed by Jesus in the Lord's Prayer, has been explored. He has given us his teaching to lead us to enlightenment, not just to help us improve our earthly existence or to aid us in collecting more earthly treasures or to reach any other earthly goals. That is a side-effect at the most.

This book is a product of the Christian Mystical Association, as my teacher Joshua called it. That is not an organization in the world, but an organization in the mind. The following teachers on my path are part of that: Jesus and his Course in Miracles and its American teachers from the Endeavor Academy Joshua and Liberty, the leader of Endeavor Academy who is called the 'Master Teacher', Greta, Robert Jan Visser, Ritah, Arty, Clark and many others: Marianne Williamson and Louise Hay, who first introduced me to this way of thinking through the program of Oprah Winfrey on television: the books by Joel Goldsmith, James Allen, Gardner Hunting, 'Lessons in Truth' by Emilie Cady and some books from Unity Church, like Dana Gatlin's 'God is the answer': Mary Baker Eddy and her book 'Science and Health with key to the Scriptures': Masaharu Taniguchi; Lee Coit; The Masters of the Far East: The Science of Mind by Ernest Holmes: The work of Meister Eckhart, Jacob Boehme, W. John Murray, Joseph Murphy, Wayne Dyer, Martin Kojc, Iyanla Vanzant; the work of Herbert Beierle, founder and dean of 'the Church of God Unlimited': and I could go on and on and on. Also many books about the Lord's Prayer have been written. Especially the interpretation of Emmet Fox in 'The Sermon on the Mount' is worth mentioning.

From my personal relations in the first place I want to thank my daughter Yvonne, who walks hand in hand with me on the same path to heaven, and who greatly encourages me. She has contributed a lot to this book. I am so grateful that she reflects my transformation. I am also grateful for the support of Joshua Scholtmeijer, Cisca Mager, Mieke Verhulst, and Lucenda, who so lovingly act as students and for their gentle lessons. I also want to thank Nathalie Verbeeten and Elise Coppelmans for their love. Last but not least I thank all others on my path, they have all blessed me.

In our process of transformation we encounter the same message everywhere, in other words and with different accents, but in essence words that resound in us. The knowing in us recognizes the Truth we have projected outside of us and it expands in us, till our whole being is permeated with it and all mortal concepts and thoughts are healed. We are happy and deeply thankful for these road signs and our awakening. Thank You Father!

Margareth Lee

Introduction

The Lord's Prayer

Our Father who art in heaven,
Hallowed be thy name,
Thy kingdom come,
Thy will be done
    On earth as it is in heaven
Give us this day our daily bread:
And forgive us our debts
    As we also have forgiven our debtors;
And lead us not into temptation,
    but deliver us from evil:
For Thine is the kingdom, and the power, and the glory, forever,
Amen. (New American Standard Bible)

Jesus gave us this prayer, which contains all mystical wisdom in a nutshell. According to Emerson, prayer is 'contemplation of the facts of life from the highest viewpoint'. This prayer certainly represents the most elevated viewpoint the human mind is capable of.

Everyone is praying all the time, whether we are aware of this or not and everything we ask for is given us. God always answers all our prayers. The world we experience shows us that it is necessary to ask for something else, to learn to pray differently. And in the beginning that can be difficult, because the human thought-world is directly opposed to the divine.

This prayer was never meant to become an overlearned response from which not a syllable penetrates our mind, as is the case for most of us now. With this prayer in our thoughts every moment of our earthly existence can be holy, until our whole life has become one holy moment. Then every moment is the same, whatever seems to be happening. And at the same time all things become new. This is what eternity looks like.

Jesus said, 'man does not live by bread alone, but from every word that proceeds from the mouth of God'. The Word of God sustains us and when it lives in us as part of our consciousness, our human existence becomes divine. The Word of God slumbers in us; it does not consist of the words in our holy books, but of the consciousness in which we read these books. And that consciousness awakens to remembering the Truth through contemplation and meditation. The Truth truly frees!

God **reveals Himself** in our consciousness as our consciousness! Truly closer than our breath. You are that which you are looking for. However, that cannot be taught, because it is an experience. Experiencing divine Truth is the function of prayer. The truth is that consciousness is all there is. And you are It.

Our consciousness is not the same as our thought-world. Human thinking is based on narrowed perception. Consciousness is not the result of evolution, but the world came to be as a result of consciousness. You have constructed the world as the denial of your own reality. You have no reference by which to establish what you are, because everything you believe is true for you. You experience everything you believe. I AM THAT I AM (Exodus 2:14).

Still you are destined to know Reality and Truth. The measure of your reality, the Truth that you are, unites you with everything, because God is Love and Oneness. Love is all encompassing. It contains love for everything in awareness. In the divine light we only see with the loving gaze of God. And then you see that you are the perfect expression of divine consciousness.

1

Divine Fatherhood: the love of the Almighty, our oneness and our divine attributes.

When we pray 'Our Father' that is a confession of faith. We recognize our oneness with each other and with God by vocalizing that we realize that we all are children of one Father; that that Father is divine and therefore so are we; that He is very favorable toward us, yes, loves us exceedingly and unconditional, as may be expected from a divine and therefore perfectly loving father.

In this prayer only 'us' and 'our' are continually used; I, me or mine do not appear. Everything revolves around our common experience. We ask nothing just for ourselves, but for all humanity.

Whoever prays the Lord's Prayer, should be aware that there is essentially no difference between us, regardless of our physical appearance. Regardless of skin color, sex, age and other physical and personal characteristics, we are children of a divine father. Though we are individual centers of consciousness who experience everything from a unique perspective, it is the same Spirit who processes all these experience-worlds.

It has been said that God is only the Father of the ones who have faith in Him. And it is true that only those who have faith in Him can experience their oneness with Him and each other in Christ. If we do not acknowledge God as our Father, whom do we see as our creator?

No matter how much we try, we cannot become something we are not. We can totally identify with the ego, with an image of limitation and littleness. But what comes from God is changeless and forever will remain as He created it. Even if we don't have faith in God, He always has faith in us. And we can only temporarily put ourselves out of reach of His grace in our imagination.

In the gospel of John (10:30) Jesus claims: *'The Father and I are one.'* Now it was considered blasphemy to call yourself God and a mortal sin, which merited death. Presently the ego still will not allow you to know or proclaim your reality, but fortunately it is no longer punishable by death in our society.

So John tells us (10:31–39):

'The Jews took up stones again to stone him. Jesus replied, "I have shown you many good works from the Father. For which of these are you going to stone me?" The Jews answered, "It is not for a good work that we are going to stone you, but for blasphemy, because you, though only a human being, are making yourself God." Jesus answered, "Is it not written in your law," I said, "you are gods"? (Psalm 82:6). If those to whom the word of God came were called "gods"—and the scripture cannot be annulled—can you say that the one whom the Father has sanctified and sent into the world is blaspheming because I said, "I am God's Son"? If I am not doing the works of my Father, then do not believe me. But if I do them, even though you do not believe me, believe the works, so that you may know and understand that the Father is in me and I am in the Father." Then they tried to arrest him again, but he escaped from their hands.'

Through the ages the holy men and saints of every religion have said the same thing over and over again and their bodies were silenced. But the truth about us cannot be silenced.

The ego always finds Truth offensive. It feels it is being rebuked and punished. That is why part of you may not like what Jesus tells you, while another part is deeply touched. Truth pushes against the conceptual prison walls you have erected in your mind. The human mind is split and contact with Truth reveals that. Truth does not need sugarcoating. That, for which it is meant, will recognize it and be thrilled by it.

That is why not everyone can handle Truth. It depends on the degree in which you shun the light. If you are someone who tries to excuse evil and thus makes it real, you will tend to consider the vision of the Holy Spirit as black-and-white. Because He sees that the evil you experience is not real and therefore can dissolve into the nothingness from where it came, if you let it. So the aim is not to pretend we don't see evil or to try to smooth it over. We do see evil, because we see all the evil we had made up and in which we believed. The aim is to hold it under the Light of Truth and Reality and ask of yourself; is it real? Alongside every evil we perceive, we lay the Truth and if it is someone else showing us our old lies, we speak the Truth to that person.

Then you have arrived at a point where you say; I see the dreamer and I see his dreams. I no longer project, because I am the Christ. Only the ego-mind projects. I see my brother as he really is and I also see what he thinks he is. For this I offer healing. I don't judge him, I don't blame him for being ignorant, but I hold Truth before him.

Much of what comes hereafter can be experienced as quite uncomfortable. It is so threatening to the ego, that it crucified the teacher of this knowledge. The goal is to be freed from the walls that have been erected in your mind against Truth. You desire liberation of old ideas and conditioning. This is an attempt to push against those walls and that can cause discomfort. You will not only find things here that conform to your old thoughts. That is not the aim. It is the aim to learn something new, not just to find confirmation for your own ideas. That, which is comfortable, hinders and limits us.

Some think it 'dualistic' and experience it as harsh. Only the ego thinks Truth is harsh. When you confront the ego with Truth, it always feels condemned, because it condemns itself.

The ego tries to cause confusion by distorting the Truth. When the distorted thought-system of the ego tries to use the sword of Truth, it just looks clumsy and ridiculous.

In the same way it distorted the Master's words. An example of this is the translation of part of the Sermon on the Mount, in which Jesus is quoted as saying; 'blessed are the poor in spirit'. Who are they? Spirit is divine, how could Jesus then glorify lack of spirit? Of course he did not. The text was in fact; 'Blessed are those who ask for awareness'. When we are willing to have our consciousness expanded, we are blessed.

While we do not understand the law, that states that we always experience what we believe, we will reject the magnitude that is really ours. And attack those who do not join us in littleness.

So everywhere Jesus went, they tried to stone him for speaking the truth, but nothing could contain him, not even the grave.

His words have been distorted and the focus was directed at adoration of his personality, making him the exception, rather than the example he intended to be. In the last century many have come forward, who had the courage to speak the Truth, as taught by our Master, Jesus.

And we, the children of God, proclaim that we are made in His 'Image and Likeness' and therefore we are just like Him. God is Spirit and therefore so are we. We have the same abilities and attributes. That characterizes the relationship with our father.

God has not created us as material bodies, but as Itself. As a perfect spiritual being, with all divine characteristics and abilities, such as all-powerfulness and omniscience. Children of God must be divine. And as is narrated in the parable of the lost son, it looks like we have chosen to waste our inheritance by narrowing our perspective to the perceptual vision, which characterizes material existence. We have chosen a very limited vision, in which everything we think we know is based on speculation. But that is only one level of our existence. This is only one aspect of our experience. We are also timeless awareness, where all things and experiences are at the same time. Where there is Knowledge and no perceptual speculations. A state of timeless bliss as opposed to the unreal; perception, ignorance, and therefore doubt and speculation. Our real world of experiences envelops everything, the material world and all other possibilities, which we cannot imagine in perception.

We are not a mind in a body; the body is an image in our minds, with which we associate in our material experience. All perceived differences between humans and all forms are just aspects of the material experience. They are possibilities we have concocted, after we made them up. Every thought has its substrate in form. That was Our Will. However, it was not our will that our journey into form should make us suffer. But to experience form we had to limit ourselves and as it were hypnotize ourselves.

And we could not foresee what the consequences would be. We only have to awaken to our divine reality to escape our self-made prison, the world of pain, suffering, sickness, growing old and death. And then we also realize what a great experiment this has been.

We have been able to experience the impossible: a world which is godless; a world with two opposing powers, in which we seemed to be separate from each other and from God. A world in which the strong survive and in which our differences determine our value.

Seen from the other side, where we perceive everything the right way, these ideas are incredible. The seeming difference in spiritual development is also no true difference, because it is linked to time. And time is an illusion. We are all unique individual aspects of one Spirit and everyone represents a unique perspective. Everything that is in the awareness of anyone is in the awareness of all. It will all be integrated. We experience a little piece of eternity at a time; the experience of states which are linked to time are finite and therefore very small. We are evolving to the realization of oneness. That manifests on the surface in our social organizations and values, in which equality and oneness are central. Nothing can keep us from awakening to the realization of our inner connectedness. The transformation goes on all the time.

Everything is a picture in the mind and is being played in awareness; but what a picture! Matter that thickened from the atoms of the 'big bang' and gives form to everything, is of magnificent complexity and diversity. Every material evolution reflects the true evolution of becoming aware. The boundaries that limited thinking has assumed, are all incorrect. Every new horizon offers a view of new vistas. There is always more. Every new level of awareness opens new perspectives and is expressed in new conditions. Progress is eternal. Every door is open. We are liberated when we are no longer attached to the illusion of the perishable and valueless that our world consisted of and when we have also released our disgust of it.

Amazed amusement is the only correct reaction to this world which we pretended existed. The ridiculous can only elicit ridicule.

And all together we will express divinity, as soon as there are enough who do that. And indeed we are always doing that, even if part of our being pretends to be something else. Because time does not exist, it is part of the experience of godlessness. Your true Self looks from timelessness, where all Knowledge is, into the experience of time. There is only one time: now. And the divine NOW is timeless. And there is only one place and that is in God. There is no place God is not. God is always with you.

The unconditional love of the Almighty does not resemble any human love. It is not connected to any form.

Usually an earthly father does a lot for his children; how much more can we expect from our divine Father, Who is almighty and loves us completely!

God created us and saw that it was good. And He has not changed His Mind, because in essence we have not changed. We cannot change, because from God only the unchangeable good, the divine, comes forth. We are always one with God, despite our seeming experience of separation. And we are always connected in His Mind. We are one and furthermore, we are loved by no lesser being than the Ruler of the Universe. We are godly children.

Our Source gave us everything in our creation. Nothing was denied us. We have the same creative ability, the same all-powerfulness as our divine Father. Our Father is not an angry, vicious man who wants to hurt us in the name of love.

When the Spirit brought us forth, He made us as Himself, invulnerable and imperishable. From God only the perfect can come forth. All the fear and resentment which determines our thinking, our feelings and our actions, are caused by our identification with a vulnerable, mortal, contrived self; a ridiculous lie. Spirit cannot die. All the suffering we experience, is imposed by us. It is not the Will of God. Our Father loves us and wants us to be happy. Though negative experiences can lead us to the light, they do not come from God. We can only experience them if we see our self as separated. Love never teaches through hate.

We can only be happy if we accept our divine inheritance again. Let us realize who we really are and let go of every identification with the small self image. We are not mortal and powerless. We are not victims of a cruel world, at the mercy of poverty, suffering, sickness, pain and death. In the divine reality, which is the only one, we are immortal and through the divine love and mercy the all-powerfulness, which gives us the opportunity to experience anything we desire, is available to us.

God Himself has placed every desire in us, including the desire for more. A desire used by the ego to focus our attention on that in which the unfolding of the divine truth is not to be found. Every desire is desire for God. We fill it in by ourselves with all sorts of substitutes. Haven't you noticed that a fulfilled desire does not give satisfaction, that every satisfaction is only short-lived? Desire continues to exist. If you have one thing, you already desire the next or more of the same. This happens until you no longer value the valueless. That which pleases the ego is always small and perishable. Nothing that is temporary can ever make you truly happy. Only Knowledge of God can really satisfy you.

However, without the desire for more, no mortal could be tempted to give up the need for experiencing dualism. For the human being who is not awake, becoming aware seems like destruction, because it is the end of all that is familiar, everything one is attached to. The special relations, that shut out the world, growing old together, the distinction between people, this limited thinking does not exist in divine reality. That is why it is a miracle, if you are willing to follow the path of light.

So it is not the desire itself that has to be overcome, for it is not the desire for more that leads us into the consciousness that is chained to matter, but the desire which is focused in the wrong direction. If we would desire nothing more than what we are aware of in duality, that would be the height of hopelessness. If you would think that that which constitutes your reality is life, that that was all there is, you would want to die in the end. Only by seeking, can we experience the grace of God. Because that is how we show our willingness to receive His grace.

Seeking is a denial of God, for God is here and now. But you must and will seek until you are fully aware of this all the time. Deep inside we know that we have the ability to experience the infinity of Reality. It is often said that we should accept our experiences, that we should not resist. Do you overcome suffering by accepting it, even loving it, as some say? It is impossible to accept suffering, if we think that it is real. Under the much glorified acquiescence a giant amount of resentment and fear of God is hidden. We can only do this if we accept our unwanted experiences in the realization that they are not based on Reality.

We don't have to change anything, because our circumstances change automatically as we are transforming. Everybody experiences limitations. There is a seeming diversity and the one seems to suffer more than the other does, but there is no real level in suffering. Human life is unimaginably painful. It looks like you can maintain yourself and only when you have arrived at the other side of the water do you see how grim human destiny is. Everything that aims at betterment of outward circumstances is only substituting one painful illusion for another. That is why it is useless to repair your situation; only if your thinking changes, changes that endure come into your life.

Behind all our desires is the desire for genuine fulfillment. Desire seems to be based on discontent with our current experience. However, every desire is the desire for our divine good, God, but man does not know where to find It.

We long for love and want to be loved; and we do not realize that we can only experience that through feeling it.

We long for Truth and seek it in outward appearances and things. However, in us is a spiritual might that shows us the Truth, when the Christ has lit this light in us and that power is awakened.

We long for power, for we have erased our true power from our memory and now we feel helpless and powerless. However, all the power of God is available for us.

We long for freedom and do not realize that we always are. We long for justice and do not see that perfect justice is at work in our lives; that our thinking and our beliefs create all our circumstances and that all the evil we undergo is only in our experience through our imagination. It is impossible for two almighty powers to co-exist. And if there were an evil power that was subject to the power of God, God would know evil and be sinful. God knows no evil and gives no evil and in Reality it does not exist. Reality consists of an everlasting stream of blessings.

Man expects to find love in a mortal relationship, but only divine love can make us feel true love. This love is indescribable; it is energy, not just a feeling. Many claim that there are indeed forms of total love here; the love of a parent or love between so-called soul mates were given as examples. Or the love of a millionaire, who has generously given all his money away in the course of a couple of years. Once you have experienced divine love, the love of mortals is nevertheless like a shadow in a mirror, that distorts everything. Love itself is always pure and immaculate, but the thoughts and especially the fears that accompany it, hang like a veil in front of it.

What is parental love essentially? In our special love for our children we fill them with fear by teaching them to fear the world and to identify with a body and to think that they have to take care of everything themselves, in stead of relying on divine providence. They learn that in every life evil can strike every moment. It is just a matter of time. Everybody sooner or later receives a portion of suffering. The best they can expect is a smaller portion than others and to travel in reasonably unblemished state on the road to old age and death. They also learn that their parents show more love when they are 'nice' than when they are 'naughty' and so they learn that love must be earned. They learn exactly what they want to learn, all in all. That there is a world in which good and evil alternate. It is for this that we came here and we have all become perfect dualistic thinkers. Without realizing it, we do not give each other the love we truly deserve. We see each other as less than we really are; we all are a manifestation of divine Spirit and excessively lovable. However, personalities do not love; that is in essence not part of a limited self-definition. And yet love is in all and everything is done out of love. The paradox here is that out of love we give hatred and limitation to everyone who wants to experience that. We think that concern is an expression of love, but it originates in fear. Whoever walks in darkness, expresses love in this way. He offers hate, not love, because he does not rely on divine care. Of himself he can do nothing for another; because people cannot really help each other ultimately. It is God Who takes care, God Who helps. Let us not ask for hate any more. Let us finally claim our true inheritance.

The love of people for their partner is usually looking to get something. If that was not so, they would love everyone. If someone they do not care for, loves them, that means nothing to them. So the other has nothing they want.

Love between 'soul mates' can be a very beautiful experience; but for how long? In dualistic thinking loss is possible and consequently unavoidable.

The belief in a special soul mate originated when people in the west learned about reincarnation. Under hypnosis they went back to 'previous lives' and discovered that they had previously had a relationship with their beloved. Two errors are at work here. In the first place there is no incarnation, let alone reincarnation, though there is the experience of it. All time is going on all the time, there is no past or future; there is only the now. And that is not happening on some other level, it is happening on the only level that is real. The experience of time is the experience of an illusion, pretending something. It is like special spectacles we are wearing to see reality differently. If the past is part of the story we tell ourselves, a holographic image, what is reincarnation then?

The second error involves the special nature of the relationship. The one, in whom a soul mate is perceived, should rather be considered a traveling companion. A saying that is much quoted calls us 'spiritual beings on a human journey'. This needs to be corrected: we are one spiritual being on a human journey. We are all soul mates. We are one. And the only relationship is a divine relationship, in which your own transformation is served by the relationship. You connect to that which you see in the other. That, with which you connect, determines the relationship. You can see beautiful mortal qualities in the other, but remember that all these 'virtues' have an opposite. And you will experience them, either within or outside of the relationship. If you connect with the Christ instead of with the mortal personality, the relationship is stable and filled with consistent, unconditional love and peace. You do that by letting go of your definitions about the other. What you labeled as lazy at first, or as egotistical, or as an inflated ego, you can then recognize as fear. And you can ask yourself why you are faced with it; what conviction in you shows you behavior that seems to be laziness or egoism or misdirected pride? In every relationship the other only reflects your thoughts and convictions. You always attract people who only reflect your thoughts and beliefs.

It is not your job to change another, but we can try to give the other that in which he or she seems to fail. And at the same time realize that their dreams cannot change their Reality and the Truth and the Light in them. We do not have to approve of that which can only elicit aversion, but we should keep in mind that everything we see belongs to the realm of time and is therefore temporary. In fact it is completely in the past. The other is nothing that he thinks he is. What is eternal? The other is that. What is unlimited? The other is that. See his reality and in light thereof you will discover your own light. See the masterpiece of God in the other and he will hold a mirror up that shows you the same.

It is very easy to love another if you see God in him. That is the road to happiness, for it changes your vision of life. You lose your fear of your neighbor and that is a large part of the fear that oppresses you. However, call no one good, because personalities are not good. See only the Christ in your brother. All true beauty that you see in another is potentially in everyone and comes from God.

In a spiritual relationship you can appreciate the one who is with you very much; but if that is someone else then yesterday, you will not grieve or feel resentment, only gratitude. Then you do not need a special relationship, because you realize that everything in your experience is there to help you expand your realization of God and to expand your consciousness. Every relationship is meant to show you the Truth. And for this purpose exactly the right kindred spirits are placed on your path.

In the vision of God we are all perfect. Everything in his Awareness fills God with joy and love. This is what we feel for everyone on our path when we reflect this consciousness. A relationship, which brings you nearer to the experience of who you really are, is a relationship with God. And that is the only real relationship.

Everyone knows examples of altruistic behavior. There are many who give away relatively large sums of money. We call someone who risks his life to save another, a hero. Regularly someone, who was trying to commit suicide, is saved. If the savior would realize, that life is immortal and untouchable and that every form of dying is a form of suicide, he might be able to give something of real value to the saved one. Maybe then he could convince the other, that suicide is no solution to problems; that that, which seemingly can be killed, is not real.

He should first realize however, that consciousness cannot die. You can only escape by awakening.

This also demonstrates that mortal divisions are untenable. Selfishness as well as unselfishness do not exist. By being unselfish your self-esteem rises and usually also that of the people who know you. It is wonderful to feel good about yourself. You will have given yourself that joy. And when you experience everything and everyone as part of yourself, you give freely. You give to your Self and it benefits everyone, including you. It may seem as if there is sacrifice involved. However, that is impossible, when love is given. The need to take care of others, to heal them, to give them love, are all inspired by God. Only the one, who teaches us about our own power, our divine abilities in oneness with God, truly helps us. Everything you furthermore do, serves to make the other accessible for growth of consciousness. But do not make it real! For every need you perceive in the other, is your own. You do what you can; for some that is the giving of money and material things, others give of themselves.

These gifts are usually directed at the body. However, everything is used for the good by the Christ, therefore every gift is valuable. And isn't it wonderful if you are enabled to give something of lasting value, namely Knowledge concerning who the other really is and what Reality is? Everyone with whom you are connected, who you manage to reach, is in turn connected to many others. In the end you do everything for your Self; in individual sense and in the complete association the constructive power of love is for your own good. Serving others is in your own best interest. You can only give to yourself anyway. That is very far-reaching. What would serve you best if you lived in a nightmare of your own making? Wouldn't you want to hear that it is just a dream?

True giving is surrendering to the point of surrendering all your thoughts to the Holy Spirit. Giving is creating. The Spirit can only create, it is unable to exchange. When you do not give, you do not create and you are in the experience of limitation and death. Then you are stuck in the constructs of your own mind. Everything is your Self. Let go of your identification with a small, limited self. Become aware why you want something; if you think it's money that will make you happy, know then that anything you can buy pales in comparison to the joy God gives. If you look for your happiness in a romantic relationship, realize that you experience love by giving it. Give all the love you possibly can to everyone you meet. And do not forget yourself; the love you are looking for is in you. Do only that which makes you feel good about yourself. If you are yourself you only feel peace. If you go against your own nature, you feel pain. You are a beloved child of God. You are a miracle, for you originated in divine imagination. Treat yourself as God would. And more and more you will see yourself with the joyful, elated vision of God.

Realize your true Self; let us think, feel and act as God meant us to, according to our true nature.

2

The location of God; what is Heaven?

The words 'Our Father' say a lot about who we are, what our relationship with God is and what our relationship to each other is. When we say 'who art in Heaven' we do not mean that God dwells in a physical location, somewhere above us.

Everything is spiritual and heaven is just like everything else, a state of mind. God is always in heaven; the heavenly, high consciousness is God. God is all there is, outside of God there can be nothing. Everything that seems to be outside of heaven, is made up, it is a simulation, an illusion. The divine consciousness is only aware of the divine. In such consciousness there is no place for relative perception, for the discrimination and the separation of the narrowed mortal view. But we cannot live in a private world. Even in that there is oneness; agreement concerning reality was necessary to make it real for us. To be able to experience a world of separation we even had to agree about that. You needed witnesses for the mad idea that you could be a separate being in a body. If nobody supported you in that notion, you would have given it up long ago.

In mortal perception the question surfaces; how can you say that war, crime, illness, poverty, old age and suffering are not real? And why would you say that, what's the use of saying that? What we call evil does have a place in the world of our experiences, but it does not originate in divine reality or in the workings of a malicious power; it is just the product of human ability to experience. Which is fortunate, because if God or an evil power outside of us were responsible, how could we ever escape?

There is no God and evil, there is only God. When we say that God is the only power, we say that Reality is absolutely good. We admit that 'evil' can seem very real sometimes. It might seem as if fate has turned against us, as if there is a conspiracy to make us suffer. However, that is not so. Everything is waiting to be looked upon in a different way. There are no limits for us. We can experience anything we want. There is no power at all to stop us. Nothing can keep us poor, unhappy, sick, unsafe or unloved but us.

When we focus our attention on God, the almighty good as the only power, all our problems disappear into the nothing from whence they came.

God is everywhere and good. God must then also be all and in all. Therefore all is good. God is therefore also in everyone, even in your so-called 'enemies'. As Iyanla Vanzant says 'your brother is God, cleverly disguised as an idiot'. When you focus on his mistakes, you will not be able to perceive his divine essence. Behavior is on the surface and its nature is temporary and passing. We must not make mistakes real, then every seeming evil will disappear from our thought-world.

Moreover, God always shows you what you want to see. If you want to see the Christ in your neighbor, enough people will come who want to show you the face of Christ. Those who had the role of 'pressing your buttons' en activating you to forgive, change or disappear from your world of experiences.

Of yourself you cannot change anyone. The Holy Spirit changes people, because only He knows their heart and their path. You cannot decide how others should behave. A human being cannot decide what is right. Everyone assumes to know what is enlightened or spiritual or right behavior, but mortal judgment is always wrong, for it is based on wrong assumptions, which are diametrical to Truth. We are here to let go, not to act holy. Human beings are always pretending. In doing that, you eventually lose contact with your true feelings. It demands courage to be genuine. But genuineness leads to happiness. The goal is not to pretend anymore.

We have tried to remake God to measure up to our mortal standard; and we made a God who demands that first we suffer and die to get to heaven. And during this whole ordeal you have to love God above all. Who could do that?

It is a sensitive topic, the belief in a heaven after death. We can learn something from the experience of people with a 'Near Death Experience' (NDE), who entered the light. We prefer to refer to it as a 'Near Life Experience' (NLE). Every kind of experience in which the mind dissociates from the body is an experience of transformation; therefore it could better be called a 'life' experience or 'near life' experience. And we decide how we come out of it. We decide whether we go home or not. And if not, we continue to experience this illusion of separation. And the purification of our thought-world. Because the last judgment is the moment we have judged for the last time. That is the moment in which we perceive nothing outside of divine reality. Because if we do not condemn anything anymore, there will be no more evil visible in the world around us.

It is an experience of transformation, when we experience the divine light and the Christ, our true Self. If we are not yet ready for it, we return. We are not sent back, because our task on the earth is not finished yet, as people with an NLE reported; that is again an interpretation from the fearful ego, who perceives itself again as banished from paradise. If we could stand to be in paradise, in the state of divine oneness, we would simply stay. But our consciousness still cannot stand the higher level of vibration and we experience God as fire. Man deludes himself that God rejected him; he even made up the myth of 'being driven from paradise'. But we never left heaven; we only began to imagine that we were separated from God. Of course you want to know how you got here. Because you are afraid that you did something terrible and were really driven from paradise. And you are afraid of what awaits you when you decide to return. We use everything to associate spiritual life with misery. For that reason we have made up a fearful malevolent threatening God; for that we used the crucifixion of Jesus. You don't enter heaven by dying. Dying is a thought, for which there is no place in the heavenly consciousness. Your task on earth is not finished when your perception is not healed. Heaven is a place of oneness; thoughts of separation cannot abide there. It is our judgment that keeps us out of heaven, our consciousness that is not whole, but split.

Doubt, fear, worry, resistance, they are all expressions of the split in mortal thinking. Moods and changing emotions are also a part of that. Anger, misdirected pride and greed are a distorted, mortal version of the attributes of God. In the healed consciousness they gradually fade. We learn to focus our attention on what we can give instead of on what we can get. We can only keep that which is eternal. And we do that by giving it.

Some think that a life without capricious peaks and valleys would be dull. But the emotional state continues to vary; except now it varies from fairly cheerful and calm to joy that can almost not be contained. The divine state of mind also includes passion; it is the same energy as anger, but does not leave us emotionally drained.

We are always cared for, safe and invulnerable. Every threat we ourselves have made. God is the only power there is and only God's laws are working. What power does the ghost of poverty have then? What can threaten our health? We can let these phantasms in our mind be purified. We don't have to pray to receive our good, because God has already given us everything. We only have to ask to be awakened and to see reality again. There is no spiritual and material world, as we thought, there is only the divine and therefore spiritual world. Isn't it wonderful to recognize that the world is an illusion that can be undone?

On earth the perceptual consciousness will be like the heavenly consciousness. In moments of perfect communication, also called holy instants, you let go of your perceptual associations and you are whole.

While we are in time all of us will be aware of our oneness and live in a world in which everyone is willing to stand by each other as a matter of fact. We then know what everything and everyone needs.

There are no more so-called private thoughts. They never existed, but then nobody pretends that they exist. No one has anything to hide then. And no one hides from the consciousness of another. Then we do not have any fear from one another and all human loneliness is over. Animals are not afraid anymore and show none of the unpleasant traits we attributed to them, when we were allowed to 'name' them.

When we know our divine nature, we will have found peace and happiness and wisdom in ourselves. When we live from the inside out, we are always filled with love, peace and joy, regardless of external circumstances.

Disagreeable thoughts full of hate no longer have any power over us. In whatever form they present themselves, we encounter everything and everyone with love, faith and understanding. We know reality and know that in essence we are invulnerable and therefore always safe. God loves us and only good can happen to us. Everything that is not divine and presents itself, is coming to us for healing. Do not project healing outside of you anymore, the healer is inside you. Every thought you have put out there, needs to be healed, until you have reached your last judgment.

As we become more aware of the incorrect assumptions our thinking was based on, this is purified more and more. We learn to use our ability to judge to make the only sane distinction and ask ourselves in every circumstance; **is it real?**

You are filled to the rim with opinions due to comparing constantly; but you actually compare the wrong things. There is only one comparison the thinking faculty should be used for: **Is it real?**

You are overflowing with opinions by comparing continuously; however, you compare the wrong things. There is only one comparison the intellect should be used for: **Is it real?**

How do we know if it is real? If it has eternal value, it is real. And if everything shares in it. Your desire to be special and separate from everything is keeping you here. There is no true love here; love here is not all encompassing, it discriminates, looks for limited advantage and is usually temporary and conditional.

When we know our divine nature, we are loosed from sickness, worry and destructive fearful thoughts. Not that these do not surface in us anymore; they come along another time to see what we do with them, how we react. We have made them and put them outside and everything we have made will come by for acknowledgement. The Power of God makes us whole. Let us ask for healing of the real cause of sickness, suffering and separation, namely our belief in them and concentrate on divine wholeness. We don't have to try to avoid unpleasantness, we only have to see the reality of Truth, God.

This form of renunciation of the world is not a spiritual escape, as the ego would ascertain; the only thing we can flee from are our nonexistent projections, so that we can experience the real world. We do not renounce the world, we renounce the lie. That is true altruism, because the greatest possible service you can offer mankind is to let your consciousness be expanded. We do not close our eyes for all the grief and misery in the world. On the contrary, we assume full responsibility. But we also know there is no solution in the world. You can try as hard as you can, work for this, fight against that, but the problems never cease. By having problems and trying to solve them, you keep yourself outside of wholeness and heaven. In this way you make this world real and affirm over and over again that you believe in it. There is only one solution; let go and let God. We should only be attached to God. You cannot be unattached to life. You don't have to be afraid for that to happen. People, who say you can go too far in that respect, think that something in the dualistic world is still valuable. They do not realize that ultimately we are allowed to let go of living on this level.

God sees only oneness, wholeness and love. We, who think we see something else, have placed ourselves outside of divine Reality. We experience something that God does not know and that cannot possibly be real. For people this experience of suffering and death seems very real, but it is a fantasy. As long as we believe in it, we experience it. Not our circumstances cause pain, but our belief in separation. Because we have that power; we can experience everything we believe in. This is how we create this make-believe reality; just by pretending. We experience what we believe. Even though there is a divine world, consisting of absolute values, you can experience every illusion you can think of. If you want to know what your beliefs are, take a good look at your world. The reality you experience, shows you what you believe. We must accept our responsibility for our own fabrications. We reject our responsibility, by refusing to experience that which we have fabricated. Because we have placed time between the moment we made them up and the moment we allow the experience of them in our awareness. And in the meantime they are no longer welcome and we try to get away from them. As long as we do not appreciate them or see that they are not real and therefore ridiculous, they keep coming up in our awareness. Everything is happening in one consciousness. Cause and effect are not separate. The law of cause and effect is not a punishment, as is often thought; it works actually to safeguard your power and to make sure you can experience anything you want. That is the free will, which has been given us.

This thought-system is diametrical to actual ego thinking. Ego characterizes it as 'unnecessary complicated', 'too centered in the head', and so on. Of course expansion of consciousness has to be demanding. Ask yourself what the old way of thinking is giving you. Do you really want the world of sickness, loss, suffering, decay and death?

Is it God's will that we should suffer and die? If it is not God's will, you are not doing God's will if you experience suffering and death. Isn't it time then to ask yourself how you can really do the will of God?

And we can experience another reality that is very close to our true state of being. What is simpler than being your Self?

We should not rest until the whole world shares this different perception. We cannot be satisfied until the whole world is saved. For this
we were called and we who have made it, must see it with the vision of
Christ, so that the illusion of a perishable, dying world can be replaced
by eternal life.

You do not do that by converting your neighbor. Transformation is
individual. If you change, the world changes with you. Of course!
Whatever seems to be going on 'out there', your perception of it will
have changed. Moreover, you will attract those events and people, who
are consistent with your awareness. And the light in you invites all to
drink together with you out of the cup of eternity. You can experience
Heaven on earth. When you awaken, the whole world awakens with
you. And that is happening now!

Heavenly consciousness is not just meant for mystics. It is the home
of us all. When we recognize this, we are overflowing with joy. In this
state which is described as 'rebirth', there is a smiling tranquility in us,
the 'peace that passes every human understanding'.

3

Hallowing and healing the Name of God.

After our awakening we cannot refrain from honoring and praising God, for this priceless treasure, this pearl of immeasurable worth we have found inside of us. 'Hallowed be thy name' is an expression of this delight and praise.

It is also the affirmation that it is the ultimate destiny of each human being to manifest the characteristics of God fully, in wholeness. We complete God, by expressing the godly. The 'Name of God' refers to the divine characteristics, not to a human name. In our perception we have attributed all kinds of characteristics to ourselves which are not in accordance with Divine Reality. We attribute only unreal characteristics to what we perceive, because we perceive everything in terms of good or bad. However, it is not good or bad, it just is not real. Everything is God and all is in God; everything we perceive that is not godly, must be an illusion. We have made up the world of conflict and suffering and death that we perceive. Perception is based on the senses and on interpretation of the perception through the senses; but eyes deceive and ears lie. In the perceptual world nothing is certain, everything is temporary knowledge, till the next insight makes everything uncertain again. Everything is speculation, hypotheses. That which seems so certain at first, is ridiculed a century later. In the world of human cognition it is very easy to make mistakes. Our perception only shows us small unrelated pieces of reality.

This godless world begins with perception, a way of perceiving that is opposite of divine cognition, and divine certainty is replaced by human fallibility. The apparatus of the senses is that which enables us to experience illusions. We can only see small parts of the whole. And the small unreal I seeks with grim unrelenting diligence for everything that witnesses of its own reality and the lie of that which cannot exist; the signs of mortality, sickness, pain, suffering and death. The fear-based perception sees all around it something to be afraid of. And all our judging is based on this fear.

To have insight in our phantasms about the world and let them go, healing of our perception is necessary. Our perception can only be made whole again with the help of a higher power. We reach the state of consciousness, in which this is possible, when we open up to the Holy Spirit, also called the Whole Spirit or the Holy Inspiration. The same vision that dished up lies can lead us to Truth. Everything can be reinterpreted in favor of divine reality. When we follow the light of the teacher God has given us, we see the world as God beholds it. We only have to be willing to hear this Voice in everything we hear and to see this Light in everything we behold. And this willingness shows it to us.

Which godlike qualities should we have? Altruism is seen as one of the most important Christian virtues. We can ask ourselves if it is so desirable, besides attainable, considering the actual definition of altruism. Behind this ideal is the idea of sacrifice. And God does not require any sacrifice. The only things you have to sacrifice are the convictions that bring you conflict. Your thought-world determines how you feel. Sacrifice is impossible. We do become altruistic, but not in the way the ego prescribes. We want to give our brothers everything that serves the transformation of the mind. We want to teach them, not only through words but also through our example. We cannot act differently; in the beginning maybe only because we see that we are always teaching ourselves. And as time goes by we realize that the experience of everyone is always shared. We experience our oneness. You could call it compassion; this feeling originates in the recognition that it is I who experiences lack, it is I who experiences godlessness. But no one is a body. And we know that we must not make this hallucination real.

Our understanding of God is now being healed. If you answer to God's Call, which is your calling, you immediately are in His Service. And all your worldly attachments and delusions are broken or transformed. You enter every relationship as God's minister and every relationship is used by the Holy Spirit to augment your spiritual awareness. And you are used to raise the awareness of God everywhere and to bring the Light everywhere.

Many books could be written about the initiations awaiting those who tread this path. And that has been done.

Ultimately we have to recognize that God is everything and everything can only be whole. But we see unmistakable evil. When we realize that we are experiencing our own illusions, that God does not know it, we begin to become aware of divine reality.

Healing our breach in communication is done by contemplation and meditation. We can get to know and experience God in this way; the divine qualities are revealed in us as the love flowing through us, a love that takes possession of us more and more under every possible circumstance and that envelops everything in our experience.

In prayer and meditation we can connect to the divine world. In meditation we connect to our Source and thus receive new vitality and inspiration. Through meditation we are filled with peace and harmony, and pour this out over everyone who comes into contact with us, also over the ones we do not see.

So meditation is the focusing of the attention on the divine and everything you do in the process is an aid not to let that attention wander. The intention is indicative of the object of attention. If somebody says a mantra, he does so with a reason. In most cases to seek contact with the divine. You cannot seek God in vain; the prayer of the heart is always answered. How it will look depends on the interpretations you put between yourself and the experience of the divine.

God remains Itself, but as soon as the thought process and therefore your old thoughts and expectations start to interfere, you create Him in your own image and likeness. In the Bible we are admonished not to make images of God. Our idols are not just the substitutes for God, in the form of attachment to earthly pleasures, but also our definitions of God. We should not try to define God based on our limited fearful human perception. Let God tell us Who and What He is.

It is impossible to understand God within human perception. With our perceptual consciousness we cannot experience Totality, but we can transcend this consciousness. We cannot comprehend infinity with our intellect. The intellect was the tool of the ego up till now, of the filtering mechanism with which we maintain this world of good and evil.

Therefore we have to let our thoughts be purified before we can experience our oneness with God. We have to become like children, with the faith of children and set aside everything we think we know. God reveals Himself to those who seek Him earnestly and passionately with an open mind. We unfold spiritually by turning inside, not by rituals or by good deeds. That is where you find the Power of God. Listen to that inner voice.

We do not attain the desired result by talking piously about God or by discussions with others or intellectual research; they can witness to desire, but the ideas of others can often create confusion, because the advice of mortal thinking is not based on the right information. Desire and patience are finally answered by God, for those who seek God in the silence.

However, it is not necessary to wait to contact God. In the wonderful book 'Working with God' Gardner Hunting states that you do not have to wait for peace and the resulting joy. The things of the earth require time, we reap when the harvest is ripe. But the fruits of the Spirit are always available. As soon as you start to look for the Kingdom, you will find it. You do not have to wait until your mind is purified; leave that to the Holy Spirit. You only have to be willing and to open up yourself in faith for the love, peace and joy God wants to give you.

There are many ways to pray. The act of praying is contemplation; turning the attention inward and reflecting on the words. Concentration is often considered a problem. Staying awake and not letting the thoughts wander seems to be a challenge. Admittedly, meditation has to be learned. But when we are willing and persist, step by step we succeed. An inner urge has developed to meditate and be about our Father's business. The world of our thoughts is more and more filled with the divine and where could our thoughts then stray?

Many say the Lord's Prayer in affirmative form. And doubtless that is very powerful; that part of the prayer, that refers to divine reality, has come to us in this form. It is the part in which is stated that God is in Heaven, that He rules there and is our Source and governs our life and furthermore, that all power and glory are God's. What we are asking for is to become aware of the divine guidance that is always there. We also ask for help to accept it.

It is often recommended to let prayer be accompanied by certain body-postures and gestures. Movements of the body can also be an aid in concentration, especially when physical feelings and movements are an important perceptual mode. You can dance toward God. For some reading the prayer is effective, for others hearing it. No matter which favorite perceptual channel we use to focus our attention on the divine, it may be clear that the power of prayer lies not in ritual repetition, but in conviction. When we pray with faith and trust, it cannot but be effective; it permeates our hidden memories and through the grace of God these are returned to our consciousness. For that is God's Will.

The purpose of meditation is to have your thoughts purified and then to leave this mortal world behind you. That is why meditation is not only limited to the time you spend in quiet contemplation, but more and more permeates the daily routine, for it becomes the state of your consciousness. Then your whole life is meditation and you are a master of the stream of thoughts. In that inner silence you hear God's voice.

The goal is not to silence our thinking. Thinking is good, the goal is to heal and change the thoughts that surface in us. For that purpose the correct relationship between the thoughts and the thinker must be recognized. You can be a master of your thoughts when you realize that you are connected to one of two sets of thought sets; one of the ego, the mortal set of thoughts, or that of God. You learn to notice the thoughts that come up and transcend the procession of thoughts from the realm of mortal ideas. When you name and examine your desires, feelings and experiences with the aid of the Holy Spirit, you gain insight into your motives. You start to see your life patterns and your convictions. And you recognize that incorrect identification with a limited small self is responsible for all limitations you ascribe to yourself. You learn to look upon all judgments and thoughts without attachment to them and to offer them then to the Light of the Whole Spirit to make them whole. That is how you attain a clear awareness. It is your function to shine light on every mortal, limited thought that passes through you, before allowing it to continue.

You cannot leave this world while it is in your awareness; as long as you believe in it you will experience it. You can only experience another world with a changed consciousness. Though it may seem as if we enter another world, we do not leave this world for another. There is only one real world. Only our consciousness and consequently our perception changes.

You can only leave the simulation if you experience the divine world, Reality. But that is only possible if you let go of the belief in evil, in opposites, in fact your judgments and grievances. And you cannot do that by yourself.

Through prayer and meditation the mortal thought-world, the ego, starts to realize how it works, what it is doing and how futile that is and gives up. It becomes silent.

Then that which is real, the real thinker, not influenced by time or space, can manifest. Divine insight dwells in us; there is suddenly an irrefutable knowing in us, so totally different from the conclusions, based on all kinds of hypothesis and fallible observations, to which we were accustomed. However, it is impossible to voice that knowing. In our perceptual experience reality is symbolic. As such words are symbols referring to symbols.

As far as it can be called a process, it goes as follows:

• Looking at your old beliefs and thoughts, without blaming yourself or anyone else for them. They are collective ego ideas, not personal. However, to let go of them, you have to look first and therefore be aware of them.

• Identifying yourself with the consciousness of everything and everyone in your experience, experiencing your oneness. Letting go of any limited identity and recognizing that you can be anything you would want to be.

As a consequence of this you will experience the blissful stream of awareness and carry in your heart divine peace and joy. You will experience your oneness with God, infinite awareness, and unconditional love and acceptance for everything in your consciousness. It is an indescribable state of mind.

God reveals Itself in us as a place of inner peace where we can always enter. A peace so filled with joy that it could be described as ecstatic peace.

The purpose of prayer is communion with God. If we sincerely try to focus our attention on that and pray with faith, all power joins our prayer. We do not have to beg for the good, as we used to do based on old-fashioned religious beliefs. We now know that God has given us all the good already when He expanded Himself as us. We only have to realize this. This Self-Realization is attained by recognizing and affirming the reality of it.

Whatever may be the content of your prayer, in fact you are always praying for yourself. You are always reminding yourself what Reality is, you keep affirming Truth. In fact the goal of praying and affirming is to convince yourself of the Truth. Despite all the evidence that we receive that Power of God is the only Power and despite the experience of Divine Reality, the belief in that to which the senses witness, keeps popping up for some time. It has taken us a long time to learn to believe in the ego ideas. Although it takes a much shorter time, still it does take some time to unlearn to accept them as truth. Through prayer, our conscious union with our divine awareness, our consciousness expands, in order for love, peace, joy, harmony and prosperity to flow into our experience. In prayer we only have to ask to be enabled to see Divine Reality, the light that is everywhere in and around us. The right prayer affirms that the good has already happened and has happened for everyone and all we seem to see is but an illusion. In Reality there is only love, knowledge and understanding, safety and invulnerability, peace, joy and abundant good. The ego manufactures escape routes to try to make the ego world real. Instead of totally denying that the ego world would be an illusion, it now discerns 'levels'. Then there is the world of common everyday experience, which is very real; and the world of God, which is still very far from us. The ego keeps trying to make the illusion real. However, there is only one level, the level we all are. The rest is like a movie, playing in front of us. We are not a part of it. We can identify with the actors, but it just isn't real. Everything we perceive here, be it beautiful or ugly or good or evil, just is not real. But that only becomes an experience, when we are willing to let go of our belief in illusions.

Prayer can only serve one personal purpose; we can ask that our eyes be opened to experience Reality again. Even that request is really superfluous, because it is the only thing that is really going on here. But as long as we seem to live in this make-believe world, it is necessary for us to do that.

The purpose of prayer is union with our divine consciousness. When that happens, we usually remember little to nothing about it, we only know it has happened. That which we still remember is distorted, because we only take images in the perceptual dualistic consciousness with us from these experiences. If you are one, there is no witness, nobody to perceive it. The Kingdom of God is in you. When you enter in, every dualism and time ceases to exist. Only timeless oneness is there. There is no I as beholder, one experiencing and something outside of me that is experienced. There is only I. Everything is I.

4

What is the Will of God?

It is the Will of God that we become conscious of our abilities, which He has given to us. In the end we will all rediscover our wholeness and the earthly consciousness will also be permeated by the divine and dissolve into it.

'Thy Kingdom come, Thy Will be done, on earth as in Heaven' expresses this truth. The Will of God must be done, because there is only the Power of God. There is nothing that can stop God's Will. That is why it has already been done. The Will of God is always done and anything that could not be His Will is not real. The self-hypnosis we have imposed on ourselves must finally vanish so our divine consciousness, our original state, can take its rightful place. And then there is only life and love, wisdom and insight, peace, joy and safety in our earthly experience, as long as we still perceive this world of forms. It is God's Will that we are divinely led while we are still here, in the world of forms and narrowed perception. It is God's Will that we travel on the road of life in conscious oneness with each other and with God. Because it is God's Will that we are happy.

A much heard contention is; if it is not the Will of God that we experience lack of health, suffer poverty and there is lack of love in our life, why do we experience that? Why do we lose our loved ones, are we ill, or at war? Why do we suffer and die?

The answer is; because we believe that. **Together we have invented a world in which these experiences seem possible.** We are convinced that this is what happens and therefore we do not have to be surprised if the blows also fall in our corner. The saying 'into each life some rain must fall' is very illustrative of the mortal convictions.

In our lives the law of cause and effect is operating. Dr. Herbert Beierle says in his book 'I am Number One' that we create our reality in very successful ways. By contemplating, longing for, or fearing the effect, we activate the cause. Everything we experience, we have attracted ourselves. We pray the whole time and all our prayers are always answered. We condemn and are in turn condemned. All the negative energy we send out returns multiplied, as are all things we give. We give love and peace, we give delight and joy, and that too is multiplied. He points out that since we want a state of joy and abundance in our world, we should flood our world with that which we want to see in it. Giving all the good we can is therefore in our own best interest.

We can advise everyone to experiment with other convictions and ideas and to experience consequently the unsuspected possibilities life offers. Without willingness on your part, demonstrated by focusing your attention on the invisible, you cannot receive divine light and grace. Vision only comes where it is welcome. God's Will is never forced on us. Why would it? In Reality nothing can happen to us and everything we imagine, is only that, a fantasy without lasting consequence.

The change in our thought system and in our convictions is a total transformation. Compromise is impossible. Of course there is confusion for a while, as long as our old conditioning still has a hold on us, but our old ideas and judgments are more and more replaced by new, constructive and joyful thoughts. Until the good finally comes to us effortlessly from the depth of our own inner being.

You also find that others relate to you in a different way as you let go of your old concepts. As long as you maintain your old identity and confirm it in others, your relationships cannot change. You condemn the other to sickness, suffering and death by seeing him as a personality, chained to a body, somebody who can get sick, can suffer and die.

It is the Will of God that we let go of our judgments, our perception of good and evil. And our disapproval of that which we perceive. Because by disapproving we make it real and give it power over us. As long as you worship your concepts, you will defend them and there is no place for God, Truth, for expansion of consciousness. In each of us Divine Spirit, the Christ-consciousness, abides. We are one spiritual being. Yet we each are an individual expression of that, you could say another perspective. And even though the personality is an untenable construction, you will always be you.

Living in accordance with God's Will drastically improves our circumstances. Our lives are then filled with love and joy and peace. Limiting circumstances like sickness and other forms of lack still present themselves, but that only happens for the healing of your mind. We no longer have to live in a fearful cramp, with the feeling as if the sword of Damocles is hanging over our heads. Every suffering and every lack we experience is a clear message from our inner being that we are not in harmony with that which we truly are and with that which we desire from life. Especially disease gets our attention. If we look at the body without pasting all sorts of labels on it and without all kinds of demands, it turns out to be an instrument of God, that perfectly does what it has to do. Then you can look in the mirror and see God. Not our body is sick, we have sick thoughts about our body. Our body is perfect. And we will experience that, if we let go of our parcel of demands. We suffer and are being held prisoner by our own definitions. Our bodies and our circumstances are always perfect.

The will has been imprisoned by the ego thinking. Although the will of the ego may seem substantial, it is not a free will. It does not create. Only illusions come out of it. When we follow the lead of the ego it may appear as if we have a strong will. We appear to be very dominant or dictatorial. But it is just a style of conduct based on fear. Such behavior stems from fear of limitation and lack of true self-confidence. When you have experienced helplessness, the need for control and dominance rises.

However capable a human being handles situations in life, everyone will sometime be faced with a situation for which there is no human solution. The 'self-realized person' is not afraid of limitation and does not feel helpless. Such a person has self-confidence and is strong, determined and independent. Because there is no need for control at all, this person radiates gentleness and kindness. The immovability underneath is not an opposing power; it is the power to surrender. Thus the fearful ego manifests as having trouble to let go of control. It is unable to surrender and brings the experience of weakness and helplessness. Both the weak, fearful person and the dictatorial, fearful person learn to trust. That is the solution the Holy Spirit has for human inadequacy. It is logical that the learning path will be different for both. A strong will is necessary on the spiritual path. It is the will not to accept less than you deserve. You cannot accept the frustration anymore. It surpasses the tolerance and makes one wonder if there isn't a better way of living. When the boundary of our tolerance for pain has been reached, we surrender.

The same determination, which caused us to run into a brick wall, then enables us to serve God passionately and to face the stumbling blocks on the spiritual path firm and relentless.

It looks like it is difficult to replace the thought system of the ego by the Christ consciousness, but contemplate how difficult it has been to learn to be fearful and careful. Consider how much effort is necessary to survive without God, in a world where everything can attack you any moment. Is the drunk driver who comes toward you slipping and sliding, while you are crossing the street, God? He seems to be able to rob you of your life. Is that life? When you no longer have to judge what danger the things on your path could present, your whole being relaxes.

We learn to bring all conflicts and thoughts we have about sickness and lack to the light. When we perceive sickness or lack anywhere, we no longer accept it as an unavoidable part of reality. If it weren't so tragic, it would be amusing. No matter how we experience this suffering, we ask for help to see Reality and not our incorrect construction of it. This is a totally different way to be sick. It is fulfilling our function. And every thought that has been healed in us is filled with light when it arrives at another. This is how we heal the world.

We live again in full reliance on the power of God, which has no opposite. Every fear of self-imagined dangers is dissolved in the light of Truth and consciousness. We are now on our way to total fulfillment.

What is the Will of God? It cannot be the Will of God that we acquiesce in death, which strikes all around us, in the destruction of all we love, that we have learned to fear. Would a perfectly loving father be able to want that for us? Who would want to have any dealings with a father who takes away our loved ones, who brings us sickness and lack, to finally even rob us of our life?

It is not God's Will that we should suffer and die. We have tried to shut God out to experience another will, a fake power. We only wanted to examine every idea in the infinite Mind and this one was truly preposterous!

The orthodox say that God wants to be served freely and that we have a free will for that, in order to choose for or against God. And the deepest fear of humans is that this would be true. What kind of a will would that be, that chooses for unhappiness and suffering and against our Father, Whom we passionately love? Everyone always longs for God, because everyone is looking for happiness. God's Will is our will, there is no other. When we do not seem to be doing His Will, we are just examining the elaboration of the idea of opposites and identifying with it, to be able to fully understand it. We seem to be stuck, because we are so skilled at empathizing and believe that we are victims. When you choose to see yourself as a victim, you give your power to everything and everyone outside of you. You probably get a lot of sympathy then, but you're stuck. You will live in constant fear.

Therefore, to heal you have to realize that you can choose. And that everything you experience is your own choice. When you confront your feelings and just undergo your pain and your desire to avoid it, the so-called evil in your life dissolves. Resistance does not solve anything. Fighting against your problems only gives them more power over you. Because acknowledging them makes them real. We do not analyze them to find the best course of action. We are used to thinking that some concepts are better than others. But all our choices are meaningless. The ego uses the idea of choices to let us seek endlessly, while we never can find peace due to the way it thinks, in terms of limitation and comparison and judgment. We think that one thing is better for us than another, but what can really be bad in the Kingdom of God? The only valuable choice is letting the Holy Spirit choose for us and so surrender our will to God. We have the freedom to allow the good to manifest in our lives. Then we experience freedom and peace.

We can let go of the experience of limitation, and observe worries, plans for the future, control, physical limitations and decay disappear from our experience. Letting go is all that is necessary. No resistance, no defenses, and rejecting every dualistic thought. Every defense makes evil real. The only sin in the sense of waste is doubting God and therefore belief in separation. You do not have to identify with limitation, because you are not that. You are meant to fully realize your potential. You are unlimited. You are fully aware if you say so. There is only one mind awakening.

It is our purpose in life to become aware. The most precious thing we can have is contact with our true Self, which is a constant inner presence. Nothing else can give us inner peace and security. Not money or other people. Everything outside of us is unpredictable. The power we seek has to come from inside us. And that inner clarity and purity then becomes the leading power in our lives. We no longer live reactively, and our thoughts are not constantly focused on the past or the future. Then we can be in the now, because we let go of our grievances about the past and our fear for the future. This gift of becoming aware of our divine reality, of our true being, is the only thing we can lack. We have everything for the taking. We are not the powerless, limited beings we thought we were. We can decide to what stimuli and external signals we want to react, instead of feeling like powerless puppets in the hands of others and fate.

We can learn to use the spiritual power in us to find true fulfillment.

Everything that increases lasting love, peace and joy in us can be part of our experience.

We only use a very small part of our spiritual abilities, as long as we use the Law of cause and effect unconsciously. Let us learn to use it consciously to lead the divine life, that is the Will of God. It is our purpose to use our spiritual abilities fully again and when that will be done, this world will no longer exist. But until then, until we remember our true Self perfectly, we are here in this world, remembering to make optimal use of the power that is available to us.

We have gone through a lot of trouble to learn to believe in the world and to develop our belief system. It requires a lot less effort to undo it, but from our limited perspective it seems to require a lot of patience. We only experience the graphic representation of our beliefs. All we have to do is change our beliefs and we have tremendous help in doing that. The only thing we have to do is to ask the Holy Spirit for help and be willing to let go of everything that does not belong to divine reality. The Holy Spirit, Who governs the heavenly true consciousness, will bring the earthly material perception to true perception under divine guidance. That is a state of mind in which the mind has taken in its rightful place as an instrument of the soul and no longer controls your life with limiting thoughts and ideas.

And then the divine will, which is indeed only our will to be eternally safe and peaceful, is done. Nothing else is possible, for what God wills, is done and has already been done. There is no other will but God's and God wants His creation to be happy and expressing the godly.

We have then crossed over to an area that seems to be situated on the border of the mortal world and Reality. From there we can beckon to those on the other shore to come there too. We cannot go back to them and join them on the level of consciousness they are on. Such a form of compassion does not serve them, for it confirms to them that they are experiencing something else than their divine reality. They are served by our acknowledging their wholeness and refusing to accept anything else. In fact they are invulnerable and always blissful. Nothing is the matter with them. The whole drama they think that they are in is not real. And we can look behind the mask they show us.

Then we live in harmony with each other and with every manifestation of life. Life is an eternal symphony and the song is called 'Love'. The conductor is Love and life moves to the beat of Love. When you tune in to that, your life is glorious.

When the light has come, we do not feel alone anymore. We feel a warm glow that envelops us like a blanket. We feel a gentle presence, always there for us. We experience there is nothing to fear. When the light has come, we are relieved and glad. All our worries turned out to be unfounded, all our striving in vain.

The Kingdom of God is eternal and untouchable, but the earthly consciousness, chained to matter, has to become aware of it. Then the Will of God is also manifest on earth.

5

What is our daily bread?

Praying like this teaches us to let go of our belief in lack. We learn to trust in the care of God. We don't have to ask God to provide for our daily needs. Everything necessary to maintain our physical existence is already here. We possess the ability to bring everything into our experience. If we trust in the care of God, realizing that everything is always there for us, we don't have to preoccupy ourselves with that. When we share in the divine abundance we don't feel the need to cut out a piece of it and say 'that belongs to me'. The realization that we possess everything gives the feeling 'everything is mine and is available for me. Everything comes to me as soon as I need it.' It is possible that we possess a lot, but we don't consider it our possession, we consider it Gods possession. We realize that the contact with that which really sustains us, the Source of our life and of all the good in our world of experience, is the true food. God has given us everything and we ask for increased awareness and sharing Gods vision.

Jesus said 'first seek the Kingdom of God and all else will be added'. When we try to reach God we will experience the unfoldment of divine care and guidance in our lives in miraculous ways. The miracles we experience when our consciousness allows the revelation of divine reality are too numerous to describe.

Our daily bread is our contact with our divine Source; we attain spiritual nourishment through the experience of our oneness with God. God pours His own Being out over us through the gifts of immortal life and unconditional eternal love, truth and wisdom, peace and joy. The material is an outgrowth of this. You can bring everything into your experience, therefore also the material. There is nothing that opposes you, except your belief that something is impossible or takes time or whatever objection. All the good in your experience is just evidence for the glory of God. It is possible to live in awareness of the true being, not ascetic, but in joyful possession of everything that contributes to spiritual growth. One only values the truly valuable, and no longer has a wrong idea about pleasure. Through this one obtains priceless treasures. The fruits of the spirit are spiritual beauty and wholeness. They, who lose the attachment to the material, gain the peace of ceaseless spiritual joy.

What do you want something for? For the feeling that it gives you. If something material gives you peace, it is nevertheless a very temporary peace. The peace God gives is everlasting. Mortal consciousness can barely conceive of the feelings of someone who experiences this. It has no comprehension of it at all. It is truly hidden behind a veil.

When we have found the Kingdom of God in ourselves, we can want for nothing. We then open ourselves to the divine and receive that, instead of the gratification of our insane wishes. They, who realize that an almighty Father takes care of him or her, have nothing to fear.

And he withholds nothing. It is our disbelief which keeps his gifts from our world of experiences. He does not force anything on us. Does God give? He has already given us everything by creating us as Him. What can we ask for that we have not received already? When we realize the magnitude of all that God has given us, our heart rejoices. Until that time we can practice gratitude to silence the continuous screaming of the ego, which always experiences lack and in essence asks for it. We think we would have peace if we had enough money or something else outside of us. However, this kind of peace is short-lived. The peace of God, which we experience, is a joyful, gentle serenity in us, independent of our outer circumstances. Though ultimately these circumstances also reflect our inner peace, because everything that seems to be outside of us, is a product of our consciousness. Everything you seem to see outside of you, is the graphic representation of an idea, a conviction. We are a story-telling species. Everything is a story we tell ourselves. We are trying to define our reality all the time.

Jesus offers us a better story to replace our old painful stories. Let go of your stories and keep only those that truly make your life pleasant and therefore have eternal value.

There is nothing we cannot possess and experience and we already possess and experience everything we want. If that does not seem to be the case, that is only because we are not aware of what we have requested and how we draw our experiences toward us. We feel like victims; a human being is totally upset about everything. And rightfully so. Mortal experience is a hell of guilt and hurt. Whatever you think is going on outside of you, when you take the responsibility for it, you let go of the projection of guilt.

If you are in the middle of problems, you feel like a victim and it is difficult to see that you are responsible for your experiences. Acknowledge however, that you must have asked for them, even if you don't know how. Healing begins when you realize; 'I must have asked for this, because this is what is happening, this is what I am experiencing. I do not understand why; I cannot imagine that I would want this, but that must be so. Help me to change my mind.' And in this acknowledgement your mind has changed and you let go of your misplaced inappropriate identity as a victim.

In the human consciousness there is lack of the good, the divine; there is war, famine, poverty, sickness, abuse, old age and death. We don't have to try to get rid of them. We only have to seek the kingdom of God, the contact with our Source. When we seek contact with God every lack disappears from our experience, when our mind is filled with the divine peace, that passes every human understanding. That is what we need, not more things or money or any material thing.

You practice gratefulness by telling yourself daily:

'I am thankful that every negative thought-pattern in my consciousness is now being clarified, erased and let go. I now let go of all negative thought patterns that have contributed to the fear of evil, poverty, pain, loneliness, the feeling of inadequacy, losses of any kind and every other insanity lurking in a dark corner of my consciousness. I am thankful that I am free to be master of my own life. I only want to experience my oneness with God and with my neighbors. Therefore I stop blaming and criticizing. I let go of all grievances. I am grateful for everything I enjoy. Living is enjoying. I enjoy my fellow creatures. I enjoy my happy, loving, joyful and peaceful relationships with others. I am grateful for the beauty, loveliness and purity I see in my fellow men, for everything I see in them, I am. Instead of finding faults in others and myself I discover wonderful things in them and in myself. We are angels for each other and we are all here to deliver each other from our self-made prison of limited thinking. I am grateful for the love, which flows through me and which I may express and for the love that is constantly demonstrated to me. I give happiness and happiness flows back. I am grateful that I can look with love on everything. I see the light, the valuable in everything. That is not the perishable good, because that is not real, but the reflection of Divine Spirit. Everything reflects me and I am valuable. Everything in my world of experiences is filled more and more with light and love, peace and joy, because I am filled with light and love, peace and joy. I am grateful because I am rich because of what I really am. I am grateful because I experience the Presence of God.' In this way we could fill volumes with our expressions of gratitude.

Every problem dissolves if we so choose. And that is done in a way that brings inner peace and happiness and harmony in our consciousness. Not because the problem has been solved, because that would imply that your state of mind depends on outer circumstances. That is the way in which the little I creates happiness; it fabricates a problem and by going through the process of solving it, it experiences joy. However, we can truly do everything in Christ. We are peace and joy and happiness. And when we focus our attention on that, instead of on so-called problems, there is less and less room in our consciousness for fearful thinking. Nothing external is necessary for joy. It is just there, if you are open for it. It is like the joy of a child skipping and jumping with pure lust for life.

Why do we have to ask for our daily bread if God has already given us everything and the flow of divine bounty is always available? God can be reached very easily and is always reaching toward us. The good constantly flows to us.

God is always within reach; every break in communication comes from our side. Spiritual guidance and insight are always available. However, by asking we open up ourselves and invite God to share His Thoughts with us. And God comes where we are; we obtain the insight that fits into our frame of reference.

Our daily bread is most of all faith and trust in the divine, which God gives us when we ask for it.

We are always safe and invulnerable. We realize that through learning to trust. Confidence in God also cultivates self-confidence. For then we realize we can cope with anything the other lays at our front door. The power and the might of God are obtainable; there is nothing we cannot handle.

Divine understanding does not come through people, but only through our willingness to refuse every apparent lack of the good and to open our minds to the realization that we are infinite consciousness, manifesting every divine idea. That realization of your Self as the divine 'I AM' brings with it an abundance of health, safety, beauty, peace, joy, godlike abilities, harmony, satisfying work and activities, prosperity, a wonderful home, honor and gratitude, wisdom, insight and knowledge, friendship, affection from all, love which you receive and give and flows through you like an almost tangible energy. You are then the 'light of the world' and automatically bring healing to every contact, because you are healing. And every mind that joins yours receives the same impulse. Every manifestation of sickness or other lack can come to you for healing. Those thoughts are held there in the human mind. It does not matter if it is your body that is sick or if you see another body which harbors that idea.

Many think that Jesus admonished us not to ask for abundance, but only for that which is sufficient, with the words 'give us this day our daily bread'. However, abundance is Gods nature. Everything divine is abundant. Love, peace, joy, beauty, divine possibilities and insight are infinite and unlimited. And the world of form reflects that divine abundance. That is what Jesus meant when he said that he has come so we can have more life and have it more abundantly. When we receive our 'daily bread' our cup runs over with divine love and peace and joy and we love to share that with others. We want to bless others with the blessings we ourselves have received.

Jesus pointed out that we cannot serve two masters; we cannot serve God and Mammon. Mammon is usually seen as the god of the world, the materialism. But there is more to it. The Mammon represents dualism, the belief in two powers of so-called good and evil, as opposed to one single divine power. That is why Paul said (I Cor. 10:21–22): 'You cannot drink of the cup of the Lord and the cup of devils; you cannot be partakers of the table of the Lord and the table of devils.' Those who attest to the power of evil are in fact worshippers of that which they so vehemently claim to reject. Guilt-ridden humans needed a being they could project their guilt on.

When Jesus said it is impossible to serve two masters, he meant that the materialistic and dualistic vision is irreconcilable with the spiritual vision. He did not mean that we should live in poverty or that service to God implies 'dying to'. The true meaning of dying to is dying to the little I, the relinquishment of our self-conceit, willfulness, and presumption, and our fearful thoughts. This worship of the Mammon is the attachment to the ego-existence in a world without God. In 'The Cup or Monad', a part of the Corpus Hermeticum, it is said that all the pleasures should be rejected which the body seems to bestow on them who do not make a connection with the other side of the coin. Because you cannot serve God and Mammon. You cannot give yourself simultaneously to the perishable and the divine. And you cannot love the perishable self, for it reminds you of the vulnerability you think you are subjected to.

When the perishable no longer fascinates you, you really begin to think; your thinking faculty is being developed and then it is possible to receive Knowledge.

You cannot unite the two. It is impossible to bring the perishable to God; and it is impossible to atone God, the unchangeable, with the perishable. God does not know it, cannot know it and will never know it. God does not know that which does not exist. The whole notion of mortality is alien to Him. God is the Good, and nothing else. And nothing else is knowable to Him.

When you begin to remember your true nature again, you will finally be able to love yourself, for you are truly loveable. When you choose this Self, you really are at an advantage. It is a profitable choice. It turns you into a God.

The Mammon is everything that is external and perishable, the whole mortal realm. And not the attachment to possessions; that is a limited and, for the ego, safe definition of it. The fear of becoming prey to greed, and fear of loss and attachment, caused people to reject the pleasant things of the earth. They feared earthly riches and despised them and condemned them. But if you have received the heavenly treasures, the earthly are also tossed into your lap, unless you reject them on purpose. Because prosperity on earth only reflects spiritual prosperity. Money is one of the visible manifestations of divine prosperity. Earthly treasures are impersonal and useful. They only have the value we attach to them. They who long for the earthly riches, whether they have little or a lot of them, are demonstrating what has value for them. But those who live in forced soberness, apparently value poverty. Detachment does not imply that one should do without something; one just has to live in the realization of being only dependent on God. We are allowed to have everything. We should only realize that the limiting view of the ego, that pleasant financial circumstances could give you peace, is unfounded. There are many rich and very wealthy people, who graphically illustrate a lack of inner peace. You can experience peace, no matter what the circumstances are. We are meant to have everything for the adventures, which we wish to undergo. And that has already been given us; we only have to place our 'order'. We cannot order God around, but he is waiting for us to choose whatever we want from His storehouses. In Christ we are heirs and everything our Father has, belongs to us.

Your financial problems are solved if you so choose. Riches, which do not come from the realization of God, bring with them fear of loss and worries. True wealth is the absence of financial worries. When we are aware that riches come from God, we can truly enjoy them. They then bring heavenly harmony and peace, for they are unlimited and universal. They bless all creation. Wealth is a state of mind. Wealth should circulate in your life like air through the lungs. However, you should not cling to money. You should give freedom to money. You own the whole world. God takes care of all your financial affairs. You are only dependent on God, and that also goes for your income.

But we do not seek God for the advantages it renders; we seek God like a lover yearns to see his beloved. We yearn for God like someone who is drowning yearns for air. And while we do that, 'all things are added' and we realize it is Gods pleasure to give them to us and are grateful, as we are grateful for all His gifts. But our state of mind is paradoxical, because we feel a certain indifference towards the coming or staying of those things, for we experience no lack. Not only do we want for nothing, for God has given us everything, but in fact we only need God. That is what we really want to experience. Anything else is a diversion.

The question is posed how it is possible then that many become rich without minding God. No matter which way man obtains or uses riches, prosperity is still the gift of God. Prosperity is the presence of God. In many descriptions of the Kingdom of God in the Bible examples of worldly prosperity and abundance are used. However, when someone has formed a clear image of that which he thinks is necessary for his earthly journey and sees it as realized and knows that it is done, it is accomplished, whether he does that with something he fears or something he would like to experience. It may take a while, depending on his ideas about the time necessary and the way in which it has to be accomplished. But the (un)desirable is definitely on its way. However, the prosperity of those who do not acknowledge their Source, is temporary and does not bring real love, peace and joy, the true riches of man. They are fearful and dissatisfied. They identify with a body and fear for their lives, their health and their loved ones. Some rich people are very unhappy, because they saw money as a last resort to find happiness. It did not happen and then they give up hope of finding true happiness. If even money can't give it to you, what can?

Spirituality and true prosperity go together. And attachment to money or to poverty is not right-minded, for it attests to belief in lack. Money is the root of much good, money is very spiritual. Money is like air, there is more than enough to go around and it is available to us. We don't have to do anything for it. God takes care of His children and gives them everything they need for their earthly journey.

Lasting happiness and prosperity come to those who acknowledge their Source, practice His Presence and are thankful for the gifts they have received.

And everything is a divine gift, including the talents and energy that enable us to experience prosperity within the frame of reference we have created ourselves. Those who are prosperous because they acknowledge their Source, have faith in the future, in themselves and in others. They allow their inner guide to lead them to people and situations that bring harmony and prosperity to all involved. In all their affairs they only want that which is in everyone's best interest. Their kindness and the peace they radiate make them attractive for others. They have the true sensibility, which does not heed the voice of fear, but that of divine reason. And that one proclaims that everything means them well and everything will work out to their advantage, no matter what it looks like. God wants us to be happy and gives us that which makes us truly happy, if we unite our will with His and restore the communication.

Jesus says that it gives the Father pleasure to give us the Kingdom, to give us mastership over all limitations and difficulties we perceive. Every lack we experience, be it lack of health or material means or harmony, is the consequence of a seeming breakdown in communication. It keeps us from living and thinking in the right way. We must be constantly willing to have everything in our experience that seems to be opposed to God, removed; not as something real, but by letting its lie be replaced by the understanding that God, the good, is all. There is no God and an opposite, there is only God!

If we would need food, that could only consist of the spiritual gifts of God. Only that can sustain us. Divine Love is our daily bread. And there is always plenty of it, we only have to realize it and accept it.

And that Love is expressed in our material experience as our eternal life, harmony, happiness, abundance and well-being. We cannot want for anything, even here, because Love sustains us.

6

Forgiveness

It may be clear that God does not condemn us. God accepts us unconditionally, not like we think we are, but like He knows we are.

Why then would we ask God for forgiveness? What are our debts and sins? Having turned our backs on God? Our sin is that we believe we have done so. We believe we are guilty and sinful. We believe that our feverish dreams are real, that we can really be separated from God.

Praying for forgiveness aids us in understanding God's love and the value of non-judgment better. If we really think about forgiveness, we will undoubtedly understand how our interpretation mechanism has gone astray.

Jesus wanted to convince us that we must forgive. Judgment, criticism, blame, resentment and feelings of guilt and projections of guilt keep us in the hell of limited consciousness. If we want forgiveness, we have to forgive first. Everything we hold against another hangs like the sword of Damocles above our own heads. We only condemn ourselves. As you perceive another, you will perceive yourself. In a vision in which you perceive others as weak and evil or not aware, you will expect that from yourself. If you confirm the image of the other as evil and you do this when you want the other to confess he was wrong, this image is maintained. Who are you punishing? People seem to be continually preoccupied with guilt and punishment; somebody has transgressed and somebody has to pay. Usually they project the guilt outside of themselves, but they are not really convinced of the pseudo innocence they then perceive in themselves, because they also punish themselves. Except that they think they are victims, that they have not created their circumstances themselves.

Who judges, judges himself. For 'with what measure you mete, you shall be measured' the Master declared. Who condemns, is condemned to limitation and littleness. And you will have to watch yourself so you don't do the things for which you condemn others. And if you do, you will condemn yourself too, or justify yourself and nevertheless feel guilty deep down, thus lowering your self-esteem. The horrible image most have of themselves, whether they realize or not, attracts experiences of sickness, suffering and lack. You are what you perceive and in fact that can also be described as; what you experience is what you think you are worth.

Only one who is awake, so to speak, knows the appearance of true innocence. A child in a television program once posed the question 'why do people do such terrible things?' and everyone was appalled that innocent children were confronted with the cruelty of the world. But the question does not testify of innocence. To be able to pose the question the child has to have knowledge concerning 'terrible things' and apply the mechanism of projection. Such a child has already discovered the matter of guilt and is a participant in the world of imaginary opposites, the world in which 'the other' acts evil. The mortal way of looking and interpreting makes a distinction in 'good' and 'evil', in 'the work of God' and 'the work of the devil'. Everything that is real is the work of God. Everything else is passing and is the work of Nothing; it is not real.

We cannot experience our oneness with God if we do not release our guilty consciousness. As long as we think in terms of guilt in ourselves or in another, we judge and thus place ourselves in the separated, comparing consciousness, which we do not share with God and which accordingly is nowhere.

God sees no guilt in us; but we need forgiveness, because we are conscious of guilt. And the mask of innocence we try to put on cannot hide our feelings of guilt. We believed God would punish us for our 'sins'. We even wanted that, because we did not want our seemingly weaker brothers to escape their justified punishment. We did not mind forgiving, but first we wanted to watch the other suffer. Because we want 'justice' for the other. However, when someone seems to make a mistake we don't have to punish him. He will already have to deal with the consequences. That is why 'vengeance is the Lord's'. We do not have to execute the divine law of cause and effect. The mistake brings it's own punishment. We have to practice forgiveness. It is to the advantage of all of us if we help him to gain insight, so he no longer makes the same mistake.

> 'If men only understood
> All the emptiness and acting
> Of the sleeping and the waking
> Of the souls they judge so blindly,
> Of the hearts they pierce so unkindly,
> They, with gentler words and feeling,
> Would apply the balm of healing-
> If they only understood.'
> 'Kindness, nobler ever than revenge.'
>
> *—Shakespeare.*

Forgiveness has always been an important matter in human existence, as this text by Shakespeare witnesses.

In the parable of the prodigal son that Jesus gave us, not only the path of humanity is described, but it also shows the nature of forgiveness. This son left home and went to a far away country, where he wasted his inheritance and finally ended up as a pig tender. When he started envying the pigs their peelings, his eyes were opened and he realized even his father's helpers were better off. He went home, prepared to settle for anything and was received with open arms. Not a word was said about his 'sins'. God welcomes all his children, who died and are alive again. We are not forced to stay in the Kingdom of God, but we can go and waste our inheritance by our identification with a small peculiar I-thought and live in lack. But as soon as we return all that is divine is available for us again.

The son who had strayed had a brother, who was angry when he saw how he was welcomed. But the Father told him that he was always with him and shared everything he had. The return of those we consider great sinners should be a reason for joy. Formerly sinners were thought to 'burn in hell'. Well, we all have, for what else is separation? In a state of dullness people do not realize the state they are in; but if hell was possible, this world and its inhabitants are the image of it. Let us rejoice about everyone who finds the way to God and let us lovingly encourage their first hesitating steps on this path. Let us have the same patience with our brothers God has with us.

We have projected everything we condemn outside of us and obstinately tried to get rid of these parts of ourselves. But the death penalty will not free us from the criminals, as long as we consider crime possible; the actors only change then, but the roles remain the same. The script needs to be replaced by God's.

When we set out on our journey into the world of godlessness we encountered all sorts of things on the way, with which we have identified. Until we were on our farthest point from God. Then the great reversal sets in, like an elastic cord being outstretched. First the lack of awareness and the belief in a world of the senses keeps increasing. When it is maximally outstretched it propels back. Slowly at first, then faster and faster. And on the way back, the way out of ignorance, again you see all the things you first perceived and believed and you can change your mind about them. In this way your belief, your collection of convictions is 'tested'. It is a process of letting go of your old conditioning, of deprogramming. This process of letting go of your own projections is called 'forgiveness'. You decide not to use your mechanism for interpretation any more and stop judging according to mortal reasoning. Are you then not allowed to judge anymore? Mortal thinking cannot not-judge. What we can do is to mete by another measure.

However, that requires great self-discipline and a way of thinking totally opposed to the current thought system.

Mortal perception is inherently dual. That is why a quantum leap is required for the step to monism, of which the fundamental assumption is the belief in one power. In dual thinking being critical is seen as a benefit. A 'critical mind' is considered a sign of intelligence. Spiritual living however requires we put our own limiting judgment aside. We have heard the contention that our intellect, our judging ability was given us for a reason. And there is in fact a way to use the intellect well. But only after it has become the Holy Spirit's servant. Why would one want to cling to judging? What is it in you that needs to emit all sort of criticism? There are almost as many opinions as there are people. Look at the world all that judging has brought about; is that the world you want to see? And to keep your criticism to yourself is a very good exercise to learn to offer your limiting thoughts to the Holy Spirit. That also goes for the unavoidable criticism of the faultfinding you see in others. Then you can truly experience miracles.

So in fact it is not about non-judging. Perception is judging. In perception there is always a perceiving I and the object of perception; a subject-object relationship. You can only expand your judgment to include everything.

When we try not to judge it ends in judging even our own thoughts instead of expanding our consciousness. But we can examine what our judging thoughts say about ourselves. Your judgments are only valid for one; you. Above all we can ask ourselves if we want that thought, given the world it shows us. If we draw the conclusion we do not want that thought we can ask the Holy Spirit to share his vision with us. And believe it or not, that willingness is all that is necessary. Let the Holy Spirit judge for you by shining the light of Truth on your concerns. Everything you perceive is judged by the Whole Spirit as divine or unreal.

The idea that the world in which there is a power not of God is an illusion, would be a senseless idea, if you could not influence the experience of pain. But when you let go of the idea that you are small, powerless and afraid, alone in a hostile universe, accompanied by unreliable temporary allies, who can turn against you at any moment, and claim your true identity, you experience that this world is an illusion. To be able to perceive the real world we must reject the unreal one. But that is very easy. You only have to take one good look at the mortal world; if you did you would absolutely have nothing to do with it.

One who has seen how ridiculous and impossible the idea of this world and the vulnerable, suffering humanity is, just can't stop laughing. Our true I will resurrect laughing.

Of course the problem is your addiction to your identification with a limited conception of yourself. The I that feels the need to cling to grievances in order to maintain a definition of itself as helpless victim and an apparent relationship with the world. This little I-thought sees pitfalls and problems everywhere and does not want to sound the retreat. It will argue that spiritual living and surrender to God is not easy. However, that is only an argument born of resistance. What is more difficult than living outside of God? Surrender has to be practiced, because for a while we have to overcome our resistance to let go our control; but the rewards are so huge, we finally do it gladly. And moreover, it is inevitable. The objective is not to destroy your being. My teachers Joshua and Liberty explained that our individuality does not have to be destroyed, it only needs to be released. And that is done through undoing your old negative thought patterns. Behavior changes as a matter of fact if the thinking changes. It becomes intolerable to you to do something that does not reflect the divine spirit in you. That just hurts too much. Do not subdue yourself to this habitual addiction. You die from habit. Come home; do not be afraid. As Joshua said: 'You will still be you. And all the way home you will be you. There is no place you stop being you. In a sense you only allow more of yourself in. In that sense there is not really a radical shift. You continue to remain you. In fact it is an expansion of consciousness. You allow more in. And the more which you allow, will be you. Everything you are aware of, has to be you, hasn't it? You are still you and you still do what you do. But your purpose in life has changed; you are dedicated to one-ness and wholeness. To totality. You are now going in the right direc-tion. And now you discover that you are more yourself, which is extremely joyous for you.'

It is wonderful! In Psalm 40:4 the transition is described as follows: 'He put a new song in my mouth. A praise from our God.'

Joshua continued to say: 'You don't have to give up anything; because if you would have to give up anything you might not have wanted to come home. Of your own free will you let go of many things, because you have learned to evaluate their worth and you let go of that which is not valuable. You don't have to give up anything, because when you dedicated yourself to oneness, everything was given you back radiantly new. You lose nothing and you don't have to sacri-fice anything. The purpose is to leave suffering behind you. You only have to let the conditioning of which your personality consists, be undone and find your individuality again. That is all the resurrection is. You just open up to more of yourself. But only you can do that.'

Finally you will not be really content, though you will experience peace. But the longing for more has been placed in you by God. God is infinite and the objective is to experience that infinity. And so you will still experience everything as a borderland and say; I still want what lies beyond this, further than this. On that I focus my gaze; I focus my gaze on that which transcends my current experience. It does not end here, it only begins here. That is what I want to express here; this is only a beginning. This is where it starts, and you must enter here, so the jour-ney can begin. Nothing happens till you embark here; only the illusion of chaos and pain and confusion.

It is very simple to experience another world. To eradicate suffering, sickness, poverty, misfortune, confusion, death and any kind of lack you only have to replace them with love, peace, joy, awareness of abun-dance and of your power to attract whatever you focus your attention on, life and divine reality and truth.

No sacrifice or loss is necessary to atone us with God and become aware again of our oneness. All our stories of sacrifice in order to atone with God are born out of this fear. God demands no sacrifice from us. On the contrary, the 'purification' of suffering brings us into contact with a God, an image, not worthy of this name. The plan of the ego for deliverance is doomed to fail. The god of the ego is weak and powerless; as soon as you let go of this idol and focus on the One, Who is and gives pure love and bliss you experience the powerlessness of the terrifying ego-god.

Nevertheless, some suffering is experienced. For to experience our oneness, we have to give up our identification with the ego. And for a brief moment that may feel like a loss. Letting go of your own will and surrendering to the Will of God sounds very dreadful to the ego. It is the fear of death of the ego. As the ego loses its grip on us more and more dreams and thoughts of death and fantasies of death arise. It is the ego seeing it's end nearing and its fear to die. However, the Whole Spirit provides you continually with the experience that surrender only brings the good into your life. God wants you to be happy and that cannot be said of the ego.

Doing your own will means you do things at random. Because you have no overview of all the factors in every situation and therefore you do not know what the outcome will be. That is why life seems inconstant for those who follow their own rules. They think someone has to lose so that they can win. Their actions are motivated by fear of loss. When you surrender to God you arrive in situations in which everyone wins and has the same. Then you find out that fear has hampered you to function optimally. You experience indescribable joy. Knowing that you are safe and living fearlessly makes indescribably happy!

There are people who think that fear is necessary to stay alive. Even a book has been written in which it was stated that God has given us fear to protect us from this world. A God who knows fear would be a fearful God. And a God who knows this world of sin, sickness, suffering and death would be a sinful God. If sickness existed, God would have to be the cause of it. An omnipotent being who subjects his children to sickness, pain, suffering and death cannot be trusted. This god of the ego was a very effective way to keep us away from our true Source. The punishing, condemning and angry God we made in the image and likeness of our little I.

This God is terrifying. Man invented an angry God, to give him an excuse to do his ungodly will. Ego, the mechanism that maintains this world, does its utmost to keep us here and a god in its own image and likeness is one of the means. The love of the god of the ego is conditional and changeable. But God is changeless. His Love is always the same and what He has given, he has given throughout eternity.

Many people believe that man is sinful at birth. However, that is only a metaphor to describe the illusion of separation. The only sin of man is separation from God and that is impossible. By taking over their 'guilt', Jesus tried to cause mankind to let go of their guilt-ridden consciousness. The confessions of guilt demonstrate that the message did not become clear, for those who still are in the dualistic world.

Many also believe in karma in the form of guilt and penance. And the law of cause and effect, the law of our powerful being, lets us experience what we believe. For them it is necessary to realize that God forgives; that all guilt we think we have is eradicated, when we ask for that. We do not have to make amends first. We only have to let go the belief in guilt. Our convictions are the seed and we harvest the experiences that correspond to the thoughts that come from this seed. In this way we reap what we sow. We can start with a clean slate when we give God the opportunity to shine the light of Truth on all our mistakes. Then we are under the law of Mercy and no longer under the law of karma.

Within the karmic program you have formed relationships and formulated all kinds of goals. You have agreed to experience all kinds of awful adventures, to battle each other, try to avoid sickness and other misfortunes and to finally die. You go to astrologers and clairvoyants to hear what your program entails. And you do not want to hear you will be sick and die. Or that every adventure you can experience within the framework of your fake identity always has to be an attack on your reality.

God has not made evil or satan. Our awareness of something outside of God, of so-called good and evil, and our idea of separation from God, from a 'fall', applies to us. Only what God made is real. This world of good and evil, of opposites, which you see, is an invention, a figment of your imagination; it is not real! Even though it seems as if man is sinful, a fallen being, man has never fallen out of the state of perfection in which he was created.

How do you define evil? You can view it as any occurrence which does not agree with the divine. But then you would have to define the divine and it is easier to word what the divine is not; words are limited and limiting and therefore best suited to describe the limited. The ungodly is centered around time; the perception of past and future. It is the experience of separation, the feeling of a disconnected existence. The separate human being has withdrawn from heaven, from the realm of harmony. Humanity has rebelled against the universal laws. Disconnection is the effect of a distorted vision of reality. This vision is brought about by human perception, the sensory awareness. Evil is the effect of this perceptual-based interpretation. People carry memories with them which are mostly permeated by pain, grief and resentment; and their vision of the future is based on their former fearful experiences and grievances about that and therefore filled with fear. Not realizing that they give the energy to manifest to everything they fear. They do not realize that their world of occurrences reflects their thoughts.

For the human thinking, which inherently is judging and therefore dual, it is difficult to deny the existence of evil. But when one sees God as the perfect and endless totality, the sum of everything, the whole, there is no place for another power. There is only God and nothing else. God is not a person; but the divine is expressed individually. God is not a separate being, with attributes like love, wisdom and power. God ís love, wisdom and power!

The divine manifests in matter; in form we can perceive God, but when we have an incorrect idea about this, we do not see it. One, who identifies with the material body, identifies with the idea of limitation. Some think that form, the body and matter, are primary. They think we are here to express God in form and connect the conclusion to this that it is therefore important to appreciate matter. And thus it operates for those to whom this is the highest truth. But this is only one of the divine worlds, one of all possible states of consciousness in Divine Mind. And though it is useless to loathe or idolize the dualistic world, awareness of Reality will automatically lead to the cessation of its existence.

One of the ways in which man can know God is by perceiving divine activity in form, in matter. God is all in all, all reality consists of God and his universe of spiritual ideas. Everything that can stand the test 'is it imperishable, perfect and good?' belongs to the Kingdom of God. Everything else is unreal, untrue, an illusion. In the first category all reality is found, anything that really exists. The last category contains every lack, suffering, sin, sickness and death. In fact every separation is a lack; lack of harmony, oneness, health, life and supply. And that is impossible, because God does not want it. Can anything oppose the Will of the Almighty?

Many see in the crucifixion of Jesus the ultimate sacrifice. 'He gave his life to atone us with God'. Remember that life is eternal and no one can lose his life or sacrifice it. You could only maintain that Jesus dedicated his life on earth to the release of mankind. Jesus did not want to give us the gift of a short, perishable life, but he demonstrated mainly for us that we live infinitely and are invulnerable. When we let go of the belief in death, we cannot experience it anymore. We have interpreted the story of the crucifixion from our fear and not from the love, that inspired Jesus to demonstrate in such a drastic way our true nature and the power of God.

God's mercy is active for everyone; and everyone is finally saved, for outside of time that is already done. Everyone is chosen and everyone is saved. All the fantasies of the fearful I about damnation have no basis. This has never happened; it is just like a dream. We have never left our oneness with our Source.

Also, let us not make a new devil of the 'ego'; it is just a mechanism to help us to experience the world of opposites. It had to function in a certain way to be able to maintain this hypnosis. We may be thankful that it has afforded us the experience of duality. When we have enough of this world and want to realize our oneness again and reunite with God, we send a signal for help; and the troops come to the rescue. Every step we take from then on, is supported in all kinds of ways. Then the awareness of who we really are grows and we will want to give up the ego. And then we discover that the only thing you lose, is your identification with a wrong, limited self-concept.

Do not cling to what you have, for when you devote yourself to wholeness and oneness, everything is given back to you in its totality. But first repair your relationship with God. It really will not demand any loss or sacrifice. The world you see is at the expense of the world in which you can be happy and peaceful and turning your back on this world, will demand less effort than trying to live in it. God has given us all the universes and the ability to experience and have everything in them. But only the awareness of our connection to everything, to each other and to God can make us happy.

How do you experience oneness now? By exchanging grievances or opinions? By separating together with some one else in a so-called love relationship? You can begin to experience oneness in a new way. You can begin to experience holy instants. In this way you will realize your oneness with everything. There is only one sin and that is the wasted time we spend in experiencing separation. Everything we see is an image in our mind; we have invented it and when we take responsibility for our contrivances they will dissolve in the light of forgiveness.

What, then, is forgiveness in such a vision? We actually forgive the other what we have projected on him. For in Reality everyone is endowed with the Spirit of God and what we see in another, reflects only our vision of reality. That is why Jesus advised us to pray for our 'enemies'. No one can be our enemy; the experience of hostility is caused by our hostile thoughts.

The evil we have projected is not real, but we do experience it as such and we need help to see divine reality. We cannot free ourselves. Doing penance cannot redeem us. In the Bible Jesus is called a stumbling block for those who hope to enter heaven not by faith, but through good works (Rom. 9:30–33). Good works will not bring us there. The wise ones saw long ago already that human existence is governed by the law of cause and effect. In the east they call this karma and they believe that they have to work for a very long time, life after life, at purifying their karma. In fact they are endlessly suffering the consequences of their wrongdoings and reaping the fruits of their good deeds. It never ceases. A very effective maneuver by the ego. Those who understand the Bhagavad-Gita will recall that Krishna offers an escape for this.

Jesus, who lives in the conscious awareness of our oneness with each other, saw forgiveness as the way to loosen the chains of cause and effect. He told us not to change the effect, but the cause. We have to let go our evil thoughts, our belief in evil and the evil image with which we identify each other and ourselves. Then God will cancel our debt. This does not mean that God is a bookkeeper, keeping track of our sins and good deeds. God does not judge our deeds. The law of cause and effect is put in motion to safeguard our power. Through it we can experience everything we desire and indeed create like God.

James Allen (1864–1912), whose marvelous books are freely available on the internet, expresses it very eloquently in his book 'As a Man Thinketh':

'For thousands of years the sages have taught, both by precept and example, that evil is only overcome by good, yet still that lesson for the majority, remains unlearned. It is a lesson profound in its simplicity, and difficult to learn because men are blinded by the illusions of self. Men are still engaged

in resenting, condemning, and fighting the evil in their own fellow-men, thereby increasing the delusion in their own hearts, and adding to the world's sum of misery and suffering. When they find out that their own resentment must be eradicated, and love put in its place, evil will perish for lack of sustenance. Dislike, resentment, and condemnation are all forms of hatred, and evil cannot cease until these are taken out of the heart.

But the obliterating of injuries from the mind is merely one of the beginnings in wisdom. There is a still higher and better way. And that way is so to purify the heart and enlighten the mind that, far from having to forget injuries, there will be none to remember. For it is only pride and self that can be injured and wounded by the actions and attitudes of others; and he who takes pride and self out of his heart can never think the thought, 'I have been injured by another' or 'I have been wronged by another.'

He who has taken evil out of his own heart cannot resent or resist it in others, for he is enlightened as to its origin and nature, and knows it as a manifestation of the mistakes of ignorance. With the increase of enlightenment, sin becomes impossible. He who sins, does not understand; he who understands does not sin.

The pure man maintains his tenderness of his heart toward those who ignorantly imagine they can do him harm. The wrong attitude of others toward him does not trouble him; his heart is at rest in Compassion and Love.

Blessed is he who has no wrongs to remember, no injuries to forget; in whose pure heart no hateful thought about another can take root and flourish.'

The cause of evil is the belief in evil, which exists in the thought world of the little, limited I. And as soon as we no longer identify with that and see the divine in everything, there no longer is any belief in evil and so it no longer has any power over us. For the only power the lie has, is the power we give to it. Fear is faith in evil, because when you fear something, it is a sign that you believe it can happen. But as long as this has not been fully eradicated from our thought world we can call on the law of forgiveness, which safeguards us from the effects of mistakes.

God's Kingdom is always there; we have to become aware of it, though, and let God be in charge. Through this evolution of awareness we will live in heaven on earth. But when we grieve or feel resentful about seeming injustice done to us, it probably is no help to analyze the situation. The solution is not to change our projections, but to let go of them. The simplest way is to ask for help. Only three words are necessary; HELP! Thank You! And Divine Spirit helps to see the Christ in the other and let go of every judgment. As divine grace unfolds as the peace and acceptance of God's Will in us, we experience lasting happiness. We live in oneness with everything and everyone and we live, smiling from our soul.

Jesus said, that when we do not forgive people, our Father will not forgive us our trespasses; before we come near the altar for God, we first have to reconcile with our brother, if we remember he has something against us. As soon as we think our neighbor has something against us, in fact we have something against him or her. For we have projected our grievances then and see them as belonging to someone else. If we try to reach God with grievances against anyone in our consciousness, we will not succeed. How can God enter a consciousness in which such thoughts are? It is not about physical harmonization, but about letting go of every thought about the other which does not acknowledge his divine being. Whenever you do not feel good, you have encountered a grievance. You are then holding onto something.

Then there is no love involved, there is only resentment left. You are in hell then and long for death. In this world death is our redemption. That is why we die. When we let go of our resentment and have kind thoughts about our neighbors, we are overwhelmed by the Divine Presence. Often we are unable to do that ourselves. Our condemnation seems justified; or the other seems irreconcilable. However, that is only our evaluation of the situation.

We can change our judgment and see our neighbor with the eyes of God. People often do not want to forgive because they think the other might think that what he did was good, that it was acceptable. To be able to forgive we have to find something that helps us not to be influenced anymore by what has happened. And that is the realization that we can forgive everyone, because they have the ability in them to express the attributes of God. Someday their true being will be manifest, for that is the Will of God. We can even take a small step further and realize that they are only showing us what we have asked them for. Their true, loving being is already manifest in the love they show us by playing the awful roles we asked them to play. We had agreed, after much persuasion by me, to share the experience of the godless together on this heap of manure in the mind. They represent everything I saw as evil and have placed outside of me. And everything they show me now I have also done, one way or another. Now I see that it is not real, that we are not that. That is why I call to everyone to let go of their old role and to realize the Christ in themselves.

We can forgive others for all kinds of reasons. We cannot permit ourselves to hold grievances against anyone or anything. Heavenly consciousness only allows love in. It can be 'natural compassion' that moves us; or because we clearly see that the other only plays the role we have projected on him or her. It makes sense to wonder if we would condemn ourselves for this 'transgression', as long as we do not fully realize that that which upset us is not real, but only our own little story. That is what you do in fact when you judge someone else. There are people who then remark offended that they would never do anything like what has been done to them. And if it were real, it would really be unforgivable. Since it is your interpretation of Reality, you who attracted this wrongdoing, an effect without a cause, forgiveness is due to you. You are really only doing it to yourself.

However, Jesus said: 'Let him, who is without sin, cast the first stone'. Knowing that someone, who is without sin, does not acknowledge sin in his mind and would see no reason to condemn a beloved child of God. Everything you give, you give to yourself. If you give hatred, you will feel hatred. If you give love, the love is not gone. Where is that love? Is it not in the giver? Do not give hatred, or hatred disguised as love.

When we forgive, while we believe that the other has really harmed us, and allow the other to think so too, that is not forgiveness. It is hatred. Whenever you do not perceive a child of God as the vehicle for the Christ, but as the abode of evil, that is an attack on God. And you will not feel good about yourself. Your evil thoughts will gnaw at you.

And thus the cycle of self-hatred continues through guilt and shame and fear and the projection of our shadow. Jesus forgave his prosecutors, for he saw that they did not know what they were doing. He realized that if people knew who they really are, if they would remember their true being, they would not stoop to this.

He also forgave them for himself; he let go of every thought of retribution, because resentment keeps us in hell. He forgave the unforgivable, by seeing that it could not have any real consequence. He survived that challenge, knowing that life belongs to God and no one can take it away. He taught us to love our 'enemies' and do good to those who would harm us. For thus we demonstrate Divine Spirit, Which is our true nature. We are love and any other behavior is unworthy of us.

Thus you forgive only for yourself. It is part of your purification. Your mind is being cleansed of the debris of the thoughts of lack of health, love, life, spiritual vision, manifesting as sickness, hatred, death and ignorance.

When we do not judge anymore an immense burden falls away from us. But how do we then know if we are doing what is right, if we do not discern between right or wrong?

When we did that, our behavior may have been correct, but our heart and thoughts were not. When divine love is in us and we look with the eyes of God, seeing God in everything, we are incapable of doing wrong. Our will, which was always one with God's, is now expressed in our actions and those can only be immaculate. Maybe not according to the old norms of the spiritual realm of the dead. But who would want to measure up to such norms? We know that God says yes to us and to everything that is real. For He has made everything that is real and knows it to be good. That is why He can say yes to everything. He judges nothing and considers nothing as separate from Him.

Divine love in us lets us not judge anything anymore that seems to be outside of us and therefore nothing in ourselves. We do not even judge the dream or those who still seem to identify with a limited personality, knowing it is not real and it is over. It was a brief experience and everything we still seem to see are old images, that were over long ago. We only have to let our thoughts and perception be transformed. We don't have to change anyone else, because you realize: only one has to change, that is I. And in that transformation I can take everyone connected to me, with me. I now know who they really are and for me they no longer have to play the old role we had agreed on. These aspects of my Self do not have to answer any more to the identities I had made up; their true identity is the Divine Perfect Consciousness in ever changing perspective.

In the divine world man is the manifestation of God in form. The divine man is the Christ. What is that Christ? Not the 'good' in a human, for that implies the existence of 'evil'. And if you see the personality, the learned responses as 'good', you make an idol of someone. And so disappointment is guaranteed. In human existence everything changes; our circumstances, our feelings, our thoughts and convictions. But the I in us, our core, that which experiences and perceives, does not change. Everything else in us, the so-called personality, the temporary and interpreting, is an illusion, for it is perishable. And God creates as Himself; everything coming out of God is an expansion of the divine, therefore imperishable. The essence, the spiritual being, that which is eternal in man, and connects everyone, is the Christ. And that expresses itself in the actions, in the demeanor of someone. But that is only possible in the degree that the personality, the system of learned responses, makes place for it. One has to give up the personality, the ego, the limited self-concept, for another augmented Self-concept. There is no room for separation in that, so one feels and experiences oneness with everyone and everything. That oneness has always been present, but formerly one projected all kinds of things outside. The limited, disconnected personality saw qualities and experiences outside of itself and thought it was no part of that.

The belief in guilt is based on nothing. Whatever you want to think about yourself, you cannot resist the Will of God. The little I you cling to does not exist at all. And whatever it does or thinks, it is meaningless. It is not good or evil, it is just unreal. You are and remain eternally as God created you, perfect and whole. Nothing can change your reality, no dream of guilt, sin and retribution. You don't have to do penance or let others do penance. There are no private thoughts and there is nothing which cannot be healed in the blink of an eye. All your lies, the deceit and your foolish fantasies were based on a false image of yourself; on your fears and feelings of guilt. See yourself as God sees you. Let go of the image you have of yourself and let no one delude you into the belief that you are sinful or fundamentally evil. And don't think that about yourself. You are fundamentally good, but you have experienced the world in which mistakes are possible. You have participated in the fabrication of an illusion of a mistake. If you see what you have done, if you are not afraid anymore to look at your so-called mistakes and do not suppress them anymore, but accept responsibility for them and are willing to forgive and ask forgiveness of God, Who never judges anyway, you find that your so-called 'sins are cleansed'. Your thinking is purified, because then you have sent a message that you want to go home, that you no longer wish to participate in this masquerade. Be glad that all the evil you thought you did never really took place, that all your sins and all the guilt you perceived, as well in yourself as in others, is not real. Be glad that you are always whole.

You have to realize yourself that you are the Christ. It is very important to take this step; seeing Christ in yourself and in your brother, is the prerequisite for divine experience. We also call seeing one heart and one mind in everyone forgiveness or letting go; in any case, it is our ticket home. The end goal is the Christ-consciousness.

For the thinking, which has subjected itself to the direction of limited thoughts this is a terrifying step. Seeing the Christ in your brother is feasible; but everyone with a Christian conditioning considers equating themselves with Christ as sacrilegious. Yet nowhere in the Bible is it said that this is not permissible. On the contrary; Jesus even said that we would be able to do the same as him and even more. Moreover, it states that we are gods. And Jesus, who identified with the Christ, is forever with us as the enlightened Mind guiding and inspiring us. But even when we are not raised as Christians it is difficult to see ourselves as perfect children of God. We are accustomed to disapproval; it is the smell of our nest. The ego thinking uses habitual patterns to give us a feeling of powerlessness and to thwart every improvement. It does everything to hide your true Self from you. The ego is convinced of the imperfection of the collection of learned responses of which the personality consists and rightly so, and unfortunately we identify with this.

And when we declare that we are Christ, it seems as if the world is trying to crucify us; but remember that the world only reflects your ego, your fake I. The certainty of the Christ-consciousness drives the ego crazy. This originates in the insight that the thought-system of the ego is totally wrong and a lie in every respect. Even the smallest fraction of this thought-system is false! For instance, in the unhealed thought-system there is the lie of private thoughts. We always look straight through each other, but we have kind of a silent pact not to admit that, not even to ourselves.

You can decide to see another world, regardless of what seems to be going on in front of you. It seems as if you have to be patient, but we ourselves have placed time between cause and effect. Time collapses before our eyes, until cause and effect are no longer sequential, but occur simultaneous. The results of your thinking manifest faster and faster. Sometimes it seems as if healings take some time, but cause and effect are always simultaneous. The miracle collapses time. It is our temporal thinking, which orders events. And when we expect something to happen in the future, not realizing it has already happened, we keep the experience out of our consciousness, by pushing it from us.

Everything we see that does not belong to divine reality, we see as it is now, with the help of the Holy Spirit. And every time we remember that we have something against a fellow human being, we can say the following prayer, thinking of that person:

God, I am willing to forgive, because I am aware that I suffer from my resentment. I am willing to let go of every false image I have of NAME. In divine Reality NAME is the holy Christ, as I am. We are one. I now give all my thoughts about that which NAME was or did in my eyes, to the Holy Spirit. I let go of my interpretation of the situation. I do not want to see an invented image of him/her. I only want to see him/her as God sees him/her, for only that is real. That is why I forgive NAME and so I free him/her and therefore myself. I wish him/her the best. Thank You God, for setting us free. Amen.

When we do not know how to handle a situation, we can pray as follows:

God, I am willing to let go of my ideas about…(the situation, matter). There is no good or bad, there is only God. And in my consciousness there is only room for divine thoughts filled with love, peace and joy. I now give all my thoughts (about the situation, matter) to the Holy Spirit. I let go of my interpretation of it. I am now open to the insight I can obtain through this experience. I am willing to release every resistance and expand my consciousness. Everything in my world of experiences is good, for everything that happens is in my own best interest; nothing can hurt me. I want to see everything with the eyes of God, because I am one with God. I now let go of all contrivances and illusions. Thank You God for setting us free. Amen.

7

Temptation—the chimera's of evil and other stumbling blocks on the spiritual path.

There is much difference in opinion about the correct translation of this sentence from the prayer. Could God lead us into temptation? Those who believe this are of the opinion that God tests us.

Of course God does not want to test our 'spiritual quality' or leave us at the mercy of so-called evil for some dark reason as far as human understanding is concerned. In divine consciousness this does not exist. Why do we nevertheless ask; lead us not into temptation? This line from the prayer serves as a request for liquidation of our other requests for 'evil'. We voluntarily underwent a form of self hypnosis to be able to live in a thought world of limited thoughts, to enable us to have this godless experience of lovelessness and joylessness. Because God gives us everything we ask for, even the power to perceive the impossible. Now we want to go home. It is our time of awakening. Let us be aware if we wander, if we are in danger of falling asleep again. In this line there is everything we need to let our 'memory-loss' be undone.

Thus this explanation is not opposed to the other translations of this text, although there are almost as many different translations of it as there are bible versions.

In the Lamsa Bible (1957) which is based on the Peshitta, of which is said that it is the oldest Bible manuscript, this line goes as follows: 'and do not let us enter into temptation, but deliver us from error'.

In de CEV (Contemporary English Version, 1995), the modern English version, it says: 'Keep us from being tempted and protect us from evil'.

In fact it also contains the acknowledgement that God is in charge of our spiritual unfoldment. God leads us on the spiritual path, but there are stumbling blocks. The largest stumbling block on our path is our false identification with a limited I. The ego is a delusion that has led to other delusions. The thinking of this ego is based on belief in evil and the fear that stems from it. Evil is not real, it is not some being; but there is the experience of evil. Every evil is produced by the abuse of the divine power we have at our disposal. We use it to experience limitation and conflict.

When we recognize this immediately a new pitfall surfaces; we must be on guard not to focus our attention on the dissection of the ego. We did this in the past with our devils and demons and what has it rendered us? We can only experience the divine by allowing the divine, by focusing our attention on it. That is why Jesus said; 'do not resist evil'. We shouldn't make evil real, because when we fight devils, demons, the ego and all mortal limitations, these only are enlarged in our experience and thought world.

When Jesus said 'do not resist evil' he meant that an attitude of meekness, which tolerates every attack, is the best way to handle 'attackers', not false humbleness. He set the example himself. Why would this be right?

Well, in the first place attack is only visible to those who have attack thoughts and think that attack is possible. The teacher sees no attack, he sees people who pretend to be vulnerable and can attack. They live in the illusion of fear. He shows them that he does not feel attacked, for he knows attack is not possible. We are invulnerable and one in spirit. In this way he shows them that they too are safe. Unfortunately some did not want to see this; they thought Jesus had to be unique to be able to stand what was apparently done unto him. He said we would be able to do everything he did and even more, but they knew better and thus the fools declared him to be a liar. It does not mean the teacher offers himself as a 'doormat' for everyone's urge to dominate. Where he thinks it is necessary he will withdraw from the ego's battle-field whichever way he can, out of love for himself and respect for divine reality. It is not wrong to confront people with the impurities in their thinking and convictions, if only to make sure they don't get a hold on you. It demonstrates respect not to force anyone to share the same faith, but you also have to respect your own convictions and not avoid disagreement at the cost of all that is dear to you. You can look on it as the sowing of valuable seeds.

However, Jesus said: 'Do not cast pearls to the swine'. Meaning, if one is clearly not ready, then leave this person alone, without judging him or her. Ultimately, we all arrive at the same point, our home in heaven which we never left, traveling on our own path and in our own pace. In the eyes of the ego the other is always doing it wrong. If you withdraw from conflict, it will criticize that with many arguments and if you want to save somebody years of sorrow and stick your neck out for this reason, risking disapproval and rejection from your fellow man, the ego will also regard that as unloving. As long as your intention is pure, free of any urge to dominate or manipulate, these reactions will surprise you at the most. That which feels attacked is not real, it is only an appearance in Consciousness. That which is real cannot be attacked. You are not engaged in a contest. You can never satisfy the ego or per-manently please it. Your popularity is always only short-lived. If you please God and do His Will everything and everyone is pleased with you. And moreover you are very content with the Self you have redis-covered.

The second reason not to resist is that 'evil' only exists in the eye of the beholder, the vision of the observer. There is no evil and those who perceive it, must let their thoughts be purified. They have considered it possible and that is how this theatrical performance was brought into expression. It is too late then to say it is not real, because it is real in the experience of the one living it. But it is not too late to choose again.

We are always allowed to ask again to experience divine reality, instead of delusions. And that may seem difficult, but it is only difficult if you say it is. Your word is the law unto your life.

God helps and that is the most important reason for defenselessness. He who trusts in God does not have to defend himself, for he already has all protection possible. God has made us invincible. The resurrection of Jesus was an all too obvious demonstration of that. And everyone is equal to him. But those who are not yet able to demonstrate this invulnerability can ask his help. Miracles still happen as long as that is necessary.

When we experience fear, we can ask ourselves; where is my faith? What do I put my faith in, good or evil, spirit or matter? There is no lack of faith, no lack of power to believe. We have an endless supply. If we don't succeed it is because we believe in what is wrong. The keyword here is faith in the good, in God. Fear is belief in evil. Every doubt is a vote of no-confidence and attests to faith in evil. When our trust is correctly aimed we trust in God and expect only the good.

Of course blind faith is senseless. Dogmatic thinking is of no avail to anyone. How do we know, however, if we are facing divine reality and not all kinds of dreams within the one dream? How do we know what is true? There are so many ideas about what is true and real; are there criteria we can use to decide if we are standing before spiritual Truth? How do we know if God really exists and where our experience is based on?

As long as we believe in evil we are in the ego's trap. There is no way out, because we can never be certain if we are not manipulated by a power outside of us. And because it will always be done to us unto our belief, we will experience evil. But when we realize that God is the only power and every apparent evil an illusion without any real basis, we will experience that which comes from God. Nevertheless, there is a criterion to see if your faith in God is justified.

What are its fruits? Your belief in God can give your the experience of different phenomena. You can have differing light experiences and experience in many ways that there is another reality. But that is only the beginning. Because then divine Infinity is revealed to us more and more. Every revelation is a knowing, knowing the Truth, that cannot be altered in any way. Those who were still in the ego's hold, hated Jesus, because he had an irrefutable answer to everything. His reasoning was watertight. He knows the Truth and nothing can oppose that. Knowing the Truth gives you certainty, with which the weak, hypothetical gibberish of the ego does not know how to cope. When you realize the divine presence in your consciousness, both you and the external circumstances change. Your life is then filled with wonder and beauty and fulfillment. You live free, carefree and joyful.

But the manner in which to go about it is: first you believe, then you see. It is in fact very scientific. You formulate a hypothesis and design an experiment to give the event a possibility of occurring. You do not construct an experiment in which the occurrence is on forehand impossible. If faith is necessary to experience God, it is very scientific to believe in God, until the contrary has been proven. Of course we cannot measure the spiritual power, that is God, through our limited mortal concepts. God is everything we choose to experience in It. The human mind can hardly imagine the vastness of the physical universe, let alone the infinity and comprehensiveness of Divine Mind. The metaphysical reality influences the lives of millions of people on this planet in many different ways. In view of the existing consensus about the possibility to experience and know God among people who believed and whose beliefs were confirmed, it is in fact a very strong theory. Agnostics and atheists based their 'argumentation' on the old ideas about God, which are distorted interpretations of Truth.

Thus the story is told that God is not the good, because the faithful often live lives of sacrifice and sorrow. But is it not true that they use the power of God for this, because they believe in a God, who demands this of them? Let us carry out the experiment in which everyone gives God, the good, a chance and then see if our faith renders something else. God has given us the ability to make illusions, but also to create together with Him; and we can use the so-called free will, of which the ego is always speaking, for this. Free will has not been given to us to choose between heaven and hell. As Joshua said: 'Every choice is always a choice between heaven and hell. Hell is comparison, hell is the necessity to associate. To observe yourself is what hell is. That's what fear is. Don't identify with the dream anymore. I will not enter into your dream. I've done with dreaming. You're the dreamer, why would you choose? You're all there is. Who could choose between joy and pain? What choice is that?

It's all a joke at which the Son of God forgot to laugh. It's silly; how could I believe I was this?

You rely on dreams (things outside of you, guru's and so on) to save you from the dream. We entered in this together with an agreement to kill each other.'

We have a free will, because God has created us like Itself and It has a free will. In the dualistic world, however, our will is not free. It is an imprisoned will. An imprisoned will is subject to motives stemming from fear. As long as your will is imprisoned you can only choose that to which you have no divine right or that is not good enough for you.

A free will is disciplined not to give in to fear, limitation and power-lessness.

We have restrained our capability to create here. Here we only make believe, we simulate. We make nothing here that is real. Of course the fact that we can imagine all this is an extraordinary feat.

In his book 'Above Life's Turmoil' James Allen wrote the following about temptation:

'The good in a man is never tempted. Goodness destroys temptation. It is the evil in a man that is aroused and tempted. The measure of a man's temptations is the exact register of his own unholiness. As a man purifies his heart, temptation ceases, for when a certain unlawful desire has been taken out of the heart, the object which formerly appealed to it can no longer do so, but becomes dead and powerless, for there is nothing left in the heart that can respond to it. The honest man cannot be tempted to steal, let the

occasion be ever so opportune. The man of purified appetites cannot be tempted to gluttony and drunkenness, though the viands and wines be the most luscious. He of an enlightened understanding, whose mind is calm in the strength of inward virtue, can never be tempted to anger, irritability or revenge, and the wiles and charms of the wanton fall upon the purified heart as empty meaningless shadows.

Temptation shows a man just where he is sinful and ignorant, and is a means of urging him on to higher altitudes of knowledge and purity. Without temptation the soul cannot grow and become strong, there could be no wisdom, no real virtue; and though there would be lethargy and death, there could be no peace and no fullness of life. When temptation is understood and conquered, perfection is assured. Such perfection may become any man's who is willing to cast every selfish and impure desire by which he is possessed, into the sacrificial fire of knowledge. Let men, therefore, search diligently for Truth, realizing that whilst they are subject to temptation, they have not comprehended Truth, and have much to learn.

In that false self lies the germ of every suffering, the blight of every hope, the substance of every grief. When you are ready to give it up; when you are willing to have laid bare before you all its selfishness, impurity, and ignorance, and to confess its darkness to the uttermost, then will you enter upon the life of self-knowledge and self-mastery. You will become conscious of the god within you, of that divine nature which, seeking no gratification, abides in a region of perpetual joy and peace where suffering cannot come and where temptation can find no foothold. Establishing yourself, day by day, more and more firmly in that inward Divinity, the time will at last come when you will be able to say with Him whom millions worship, few understand and fewer still follow,—'The Prince of this world cometh and hath nothing in me.'

That which in us is an attack on God, which wants to maintain this godless world, our identification with an embodied, separate, weak I, tries in different subtle ways to maintain the situation as it is. The further we advance on the path to realization of our true Self, the more concealed the obstacles in us are. Look at that to which you are still clinging. What do you think you need? What is it that thinks it has to survive? A physical identity? Your relationships with others? Every thought you have has all power at its disposal. You must take responsibility for that which you want to be. Do you want to be something different from what God created? No one will stop you.

In this transformation we go through periods in which everything seems to be upside down. You are losing your frame of reference, everything you identified with at first. Everything is unsettled. And, moreover, our fear thoughts keep getting more and more subtle.

Realize that everything is in you and is immediately achievable in the here-and-now. That that would not be so is one of the most subtle illusions; as long as we believe that something is outside of our reach, that is so, whether it is a material goal or the spiritual experience.

During the first stage of our purification tears can flow lavishly. In the beginning stages of your purification you may feel an indescribably deep sorrow, as if you mourn for the whole universe. But nevertheless we feel better and better. The tears which flow during our transformation remove sorrow from many years. Science tells us the chemical composition of tears of joy, tears of sorrow and tears caused by peeling onions is totally different. Your body also becomes aligned with the thoughts that have a higher vibration; at least, if you keep thinking this way. Else it becomes very uncomfortable for you. If you change your level of vibration constantly, your physical system can hardly handle that and you also notice that. You cannot abide in two thought worlds.

Then there comes a moment in which the Holy Spirit takes you to an experience of oneness with God. It is possible that you then experience the fear of letting go of your old identity, because the experience does not fit within your limited self-definition. However, it could also be filled with love. Then you have let go, if only for a moment, of your frame of reference and your resistance.

In the first stage of our transformation we have become aware of our thoughts; we have learned to watch them and we know which ones are an attack on our divine reality. In the meantime our Spiritual Guidance takes care that we don't have to stomach more than we can handle. Because we need a lot of encouragement in this stage, every correct insight is heavily reinforced.

We all arrive at a moment, however, in which the 'honeymoon' is over and we have to learn to control our fearful thoughts. Now we are confronted with that which our reaction to our thoughts brings into our experience. All mortal thoughts come by in one form or another and depending on the way we handle them, they remain or disappear from our experience. This is a temptation we cannot avoid. And if we are not alert our fear thoughts become manifest. We need help to be alert. God does not judge, we receive everything we ask for. So we ask Him now to help us to become conscious of our false creations and undo them and give us that which facilitates our awakening to our oneness and divine reality. The Holy Spirit can then deliver us from our evil thoughts, for we have expressly requested that.

Ultimately we have to forgive ourselves and God for the horrible occurrences and images in our world of experience. How do you forgive yourself your false creations? By seeing that is not real, never could be real and is just ridiculous. And then you don't want to have anything to do with it. Not even with the so-called good.

You are innocent. You came here to work out an idea, to see how that would be. The idea of separation. But it is an impossible idea. There is only God. Everything is in God. Everything is God. And God is in everything.

In every situation you can ask yourself; what blessing does this contain? This question indicates that you believe there is blessing in everything and it will be done unto you as you believe.

On the way to consciousness-raising you pay more and more attention to the things you say to yourself and others, because you become aware that they reflect your convictions. Your words have all the power of the universe. Especially 'I am'. When you say 'I am sick' and truly believe that that is so, the Universal Mind says 'good'. You are allowed 'to be' anything you want. And in this way you create the experience of disease. You, a perfect spiritual being, cannot be sick. The same is true of every state of mind. Everyone who experiences the world of opposites, should really be depressed.

But the sensitivity varies; those who sense that it is not a normal state, cannot be anything but depressed. And as soon as they turn to the right authority for help it comes in ways they can understand. Because God comes where we are. Then the intense process of transformation begins, for the plan for their awakening and fulfillment is immediately activated.

We then follow the shortened divine curriculum. And we learn to live without making plans. As long as it seems necessary you make plans. The more you let Christ into your life, the less you feel the need to make plans. Sometimes you make a plan and it seems as if there is a 'blackout'; suddenly your intention is wiped from your mind, until the opportunity is gone.

Living without planning does not mean you don't have to do anything anymore. As you go along, you only learn to involve your Guidance in everything you want to undertake and to let go of the results. You go with the flow of life.

It also seems as if your sensitivity for unpleasant circumstances which used to seem trivial, now increases and as if every trespass by you is immediately punished. That is because cause and effect are not apart. And in your transformation-process they come closer together, because you put less and less time between them.

We should realize that health is spiritual. It does not consist of a physically healthy body. That is merely the result of your convictions. Thinking you are living in a perishable body is already all the sickness there is. That is why an aspect of supposed disease is that the experience is permitted. It is not real anyway. And personally I know people who are labeled as sick because they move about in a wheelchair, but who are in better spiritual health than a lot of other supposedly healthy people.

Yet the question is asked constantly: how can you deal with an experience of disease? The answer is: in the same way you deal with every experience of lack. If you do not want to continue the experience, or if you do not want to attract things you fear, then you start by acknowledging that you are responsible for everything you see, hear, feel and think, in short, for everything in your world of experience. Consequently you also have the power to change those things. You do not change them by fixing them from the outside.

So we don't have to look for healing outside of ourselves. Everything outside of us can be used to bring us healing, nevertheless. Everything we attach faith and value to, people, amulets, all our magical medicines and medical treatments. However, it is the power in each of us, that heals us. Becoming whole is always spiritual. Just as forgiveness overlooks all sins that were never really committed, healing removes illusions of sickness, which never really occurred. The body is made of light and is a perfect spiritual idea.

You are never healed through the power of another, but through your own opening to the power and omnipresence of God. Those who realize that, then have the potentiality to heal every sickness or problem. Those who do not realize it, can be healed by their belief in another for now.

You attract experiences by imagining in your mind how they occur. If you also react with a strong emotion, like fear or joy on those images, the experience has been realized in the invisible. Because the emotion strengthens the thought-forms. The last step is expecting them. Everyone who is convinced this will happen to him or her, draws it close and holds it as it surfaces. You can very easily examine how this works. Which fearful projection of yours have you experienced? Examine with sincerity how this process went. Only if it is an experience from your childhood it is more difficult to investigate. Because even though children also follow a program for their lives, they realize this at first mainly in agreement with the fears and expectations of their parents and principal caretakers. That is why they can suddenly change a lot and go on a totally different course as soon as they leave the parental home.

So your hearts desires are fulfilled. What you really want, comes to you. Everything you really don't want, also comes to you. Do you want to know what your are asking for? Look at your experiences and you will see what you are asking for. The question is to find out how you ask for this and how you can change your 'order'. The use of the word 'order' naturally does not imply we could be able to command God. When we ask for the good, we do God's Will. We then in fact follow His commands.

Every feeling of discontent is a sign you are drawing something to you that you don't want. Negative feelings let you know that you are bringing in the undesirable. In this way you can know that you are drawing to you in thought, word or deed that which you do not want. And as long as you feel concern or feel the pain of it, it keeps coming. Every emotion is a signal from which you can determine what you are creating for yourself. The work that is done in you has the aim of making you feel good about that which is meant for you, in order for you to only draw those experiences to you which promote your transformation. In this way you learn to control your thoughts and to determine which ones you keep and which ones you bring to the light. If you withhold your negative thoughts the attention they flourish on, and let them be replaced by positive thoughts, limitations automatically disappear from your experience.

When we are not conscious of the way in which we shape our experiences, we completely live through every experience we draw to ourselves; we undergo all possible aspects of them. And we notice; everything passes, this too. But this is not the way we want to continue on our earthly journey anymore. We have suffered enough, we don't want to live in fear any longer. An argument in favor of dualism often presented is that the experience of evil would be necessary to know and appreciate the good. The truly good has no opposite, however. It is unlimited and all-encompassing. We no longer need the supposed evil, problems, to experience the supposed good. You don't have to torture yourself to experience how pleasant it is when it stops. But as soon as you feel pain you can receive help, so the experience does not have to be repeated. That is why we must become conscious that thinking is creating and how we can create in accordance with our true being. You have to let fear be undone, in order not to draw things you fear unto you. If, for instance, you have been afraid of a certain disease for years, you can undo your 'order' by feeling it completely as soon as you become aware of your fear and ask for divine help. It is no guarantee that the experience will not surface, but in any case at least you can loosen the grip the fear had on you. And grow to the realization that nothing can really happen to you, that you are eternally safe.

If you have the feeling that things are not right the way they are, you are in fact maintaining them. Remember that even though you experience them, you are not that. You can experience sickness, but you cannot be sick. When you identify with your body you in fact focus your attention on a source outside of you, which makes sure that you cannot experience freedom. Body-identification serves to experience no health and vitality. You are then stuck in the belief in the cycle of sickness and death. This is how the ego keeps you in the experience of limitation. When you focus your attention on your beliefs, your body only shows you the beliefs you still have. It is a mirror for your thinking. All painful concepts in your thinking about yourself, in your self-image, are represented in your body. Every disease is a consequence of that. Physical complaints are the manifestation in your body of grief and resistance or expectations, things you have fantasized about or feared.

If such an experience surfaced, we therefore said; 'I am experiencing sickness, but it is a hallucination. For in essence I can only be healthy. This is no sickness, it is physical transformation. The body is an image in my mind and my thinking is changing, therefore the body also has to change. I do not hate anything occurring in my body, because it seems as if my belly aches, but I am convinced that God is working in that which seems to be my belly.

God is everywhere and therefore also in my belly. God is everything. And no matter how my body seems to be playing up, I just contradict every symptom of disease. God knows no belly ache and therefore it is not real.' And of course help of the Holy Spirit is requested first to replace these unreal images with the reality of perfect health. And that is done, we are permeated by this knowledge and we anticipate this, filled with gladness.

Even science has been forced to acknowledge in the meantime that happiness and laughter influence the body favorably, while negative emotions do the opposite. In fact we set our body free through love, by acknowledging that the problems are caused by our own thoughts which we have misdirected. We realize with joy that there is only perfection and that we only have been something else in thought for a moment. We are eternally perfect. Fortunately we could do nothing to change our perfection or that of another. We used to be chained to our convictions and the terrible pictures they showed us, by love 'till death do us part'; now we love them to life. Finally we only feel gratitude.

It may seem as if you are deluding yourself when you affirm that you are healthy and whole, that you live in abundance in the divine world, while the senses clearly indicate that you are in the middle of the experience of lack. You cannot see the divine reality of abundance of all good as long as you believe what your senses dish you up. Every lack you see represents your old belief in lack. The only way to heal it, to experience Reality, is to convince yourself again of wholeness and perfection. God is present in everything and everyone. Everything you see that is a denial of that is present in your perception and nowhere else.

The murderer is the portrayal of your belief in murder. The thief represents your belief in theft. Do not think evil of another, for it is only your evil you see in the other. Since we are used to think evil of others, we need help to change our thoughts very frequently. We cannot do this by ourselves. The only helpful thing is to become aware of it and ask the Holy Spirit for help. This is the only way to overcome our conditioning. We have to become aware of all problems and worries in our thinking. Not to think about them and feel them time and again; when we have asked for help we experience that they are blown away like feathers.

This is how we are healed, not merely from disease, but from our belief in disease. That is the miracle!

What God has done for me, He naturally can do for others also. That is why I want to testify. But only in such a way that does not make pain and suffering, the old stories, real. For as the one who is called 'Master Teacher' at Endeavor Academy teaches: 'A miracle cannot be verified in perception. Confirmation of the miracle is the denial of the miracle. A miracle of healing implies that sickness would exist and that idea is an attack on God.'

Sickness is the weapon of the ego to separate you from God and other people. Do not give it power over you, unless the experience is still valuable to you. It is weak and powerless, if you don't believe in it. The ego gets us to give in to sickness by attaching a 'reward' to it. You can call that profit from sickness. Therefore do not let those who represent the ego thinking come close to you when you are having an experience of physical transformation. In the world of humans sickness often brings attention or a period of rest or some other advantage. Mainly because humans are not aware that they can have everything, including attention and rest, without paying any price. Reject every advantage and it will be easy to say no to sickness. However, this does not entail for instance refusing sick benefit. It may be a gift from the Light, an opportunity for reflection. Moreover, it appears as if you have enough trouble with the healing of your thoughts about your body. Whatever your choice may be, be aware it is a choice. There is no health which knows an opposite, the body is always whole and perfect. It is not good or bad to be ill, it just is not real. And it is not better or worse than any other mortal limitation.

The body is the weapon of the ego, until it is brought completely under the guidance of the Holy Spirit.

The ego does everything to stay in control of you. We have attributed limited, mortal qualities to our body to prevent raising our consciousness, in order to experience this impossible thought construct, the dualistic world.

When we start on the path of initiation, this lower unreal self plays up and makes you feel miserable. And if you say 'I am sick' or 'I am poor, alone, vulnerable, in danger, fat, ugly, unloved' that is so because you say so and you believe it. The body expresses what man believes about himself. Man believes he is a mortal vulnerable being and that is what his body shows him. This collective consciousness is chiseled in the mind of every individual. The projection of the thought of ourselves as living in a perishable body is the cornerstone of mortal thinking. When we realize that God has another and perfect image of us and that that which our senses try to delude us into believing, we begin to experience more and more that our body also transforms. It could not be otherwise. The body is part of your self-concept and when that changes, when your thoughts about yourself change, your body has to change also. And this is not about losing some supposed overweight. That is typically a mortal interpretation of an ideal body. God is really not concerned with the size of our waist!

When we believe we are immortal, invulnerable and health itself, our bodies have to begin to express that. People who are in this process nevertheless often experience disease; the old thoughts again come by for healing. Remember the example of the rubber band that is stretched to the max and then returns. What you first saw on the way to the point farthest away from God, now resurfaces for you. That is necessary for deprogramming. You now take all old thoughts, in which you believed, to the light. In this way you contribute to the healing of the collective mortal thought world. The body is part of how we see ourselves. If we see ourselves differently, our body-image also has to change. Complete transformation of the body is part of the resurrection. We want to experience immortality in this body, not merely after death. Is that possible? The answer is a resounding yes. After our 'rebirth' our body is also reborn. Every cell and every atom of it gets filled with divine light during this experience and we are guided by our inner being to remain as much as possible in this experience. Yet the purpose is to lay aside the material body in the end, for it remains a limitation. Many worlds open for us, which we cannot enter as long as we consider ourselves as heavy, dense and visible for other material beings. That is why we leave quietly and without any turmoil, when we are ready.

As you are healed, that is reflected in the circumstances of your life. Then the body cannot be sick. For onlookers it may seem sick sometimes, but that is the transformation process it undergoes through the changes in the body-consciousness. And even that is part of the dream; because the only thing that really changes is the perception of the body. Our bodies are always divinely perfect. By letting go of the old body-image the Truth about the real body can become more and more visible. The supposed 'sickness' is then an exteriorization of the conflict that can occur in consciousness during such a transition. The whole physical experience changes and that does not happen without resistance. But the one who is going through this process somehow always becomes aware what is really going on and they will not consider themselves sick.

Therefore do not be concerned with what your body does or looks like. It does what it does perfectly. It is sick or healthy and every state it is in is an opportunity to transform your self-image, to become conscious of your true being. Look with love and understanding at the concepts in your thought world. If you look at them, you no longer have to saddle your body with them. When you let go of your story about your body, your perception changes and therefore so does your body. Maybe not in accordance with current fashion trends, but in accordance with the state of relaxation in your thinking. You then look in the mirror and realize you are beholding perfection. You then realize as you look into your eyes: 'I am a reflection of God!'

You can only look with love at yourself then, with delight and tenderness. You are love and when you realize that, you can only give love. As well to yourself.

We experience what we believe. For those who believe that much eating and fondness of sweets makes fat, the evidence for that will be abundant. If you believe that you catch the flu every year, it will seem as if you have a subscription. Many believe that you gain weight from eating much and heavy food. That often seems to be the case. But some people can eat anything they want without gaining an ounce. How does that happen?

You can look for the answer in genetic differences, but the real cause is the way you view yourself. Day in day out your thought patterns form your life and your body. Many have a love-hate relationship with their bodies. Their negative patterns refrain them from loving their body. They project their discontent about themselves onto their bodies. And they believe everything they are told about sickness and aging.

Many people who went through programs like those from Louise Hay, form the proof that after deprogramming people can really eat anything they want without gaining an ounce.

It is not the size of your body or your weight that can determine your happiness. We do anything to be happy. Let us be it now and not wait until the body is healthy. Are you free if your body is healthy or if you have the perfect waist? Or if you have a lot of money? A healthy body is no guarantee for happiness. The experience of a sick and painful body is an attempt to keep your mind outside divine reality and the divine light that is always all around you. For those who have ears to hear: pain and pleasure have the same function.

As long as you identify with a body, you are concerned with survival, health and pleasure. In the mortal world there is no difference between pain and pleasure. In mortal thinking the body is a source of worry and fear.

Your body is an instrument to experience this world and does that perfectly. Everything you see in it is an experience that apparently was very attractive for you. The point of experiences here is that we can try them out until we really don't want them anymore and that we learn how we can draw other experiences to us.

Your body is in agreement with your self-concept, your inner image of your body and what you think of it. That usually depends on current norms regarding the physical appearance. In this way your body expresses how you think about yourself, including all your negative convictions about yourself and your body. Your negative thoughts are old, corroded patterns in which you relapse again and again.

In order to change that, a complete thought reversal is necessary. The aim is to replace all your negative thoughts by positive ones.

Positive thoughts are not at all what people think they are. For most positive thoughts are not positive at all. They contain an opposite, so the negative thoughts are maintained. Therefore they can resurface any moment. Moreover, every conviction is also maintained by other, so-called supporting thoughts. If for instance you believe that you are too fat, it is no use trying to change that in a conviction that you are thin. If you don't approve of yourself just the way you are, there is no guarantee that that will change when you have the desired measurements. If you want your body to be different, you are not at peace with it. You then do not enjoy it enough. Let your body be just like it is. If you accept your body, you appreciate yourself, for your body expresses the way you feel about yourself.

You have the body you wanted, to learn the things you wanted to learn in your life. Everything that is painful for us, can help us to look for our true self. As soon as we begin to remember who we really are, our convictions about ourselves change and therefore also our body-image. The body then is no longer sick or healthy, thin or fat, it is only a useful instrument for our transformation. That is why we can love our bodies, regardless of the state it is in.

If you would want something about your body to be different, you could ask yourself why. Why do you think you would be happier if your body was fatter, thinner, taller, shorter or whatever? You don't have to concern yourself with what you would like to change about it, for that actually perpetuates the situation. Inside you are constantly telling yourself then that your body does not measure up. And so you stay in that experience. Everything you see in your body is only a symptom of another complaint. It is your mind that has to be healed. And you will know that that is done, when joy and peace flow through you.

You did not think: 'now I will make my body fat or skinny or sick or handicapped.' You felt sorrow and resistance and you have tried for so long to push it out of your consciousness that it had to manifest in another part of you, your body.

Every resistance always comes to the surface, so you can look at it. That does not mean that you have to continuously grovel in self-pity and wallow in sorrow. You can only lack something by drawing it to you, by attuning to it.

Look at your world. What are you attuned to? What have you drawn to you in your experience?

Ask yourself which experiences you want more often and hold onto them in your mind. Think of them and be grateful for them. Count your blessings. If nothing in your body functions properly anymore, you can still be grateful for your breathing or maybe just for your consciousness.

Then look into the mirror without telling yourself how you should look and meet the eyes of God. Try it. How would you feel if you would do that? Let go of every judgment that says that you are too skinny or too fat, too old or too young, too short, too tall, sick, this is ugly, that is wrong and all your condemning destructive comment. Do not wait for your body to become perfect, for perfection does not last long, as long as you hold onto this place of mortality in your consciousness. And what does it give you anyway? Why would you want to be 'slim' whatever that may be. You may say that you are then able to buy the clothes you would like to wear. But for what reason do you want to wear those particular clothes? Is it not to present a certain image? And what do you want to achieve by that?

Do not wait for something outside of you to be happy. Happiness is in you, it does not arise out of something outside of you. It is joy for living, thankfulness, love and radiant peace, flowing through you when you see the divine in everything. Without judging you really live, you live in the glorious present.

You are the embodiment of all that is divine; every atom of your body and your being is filled with light, power, beauty, health, love, peace, vitality and joy of God. Let go of all delusions about your body.

If something hinders you, you only have to raise your consciousness by focusing your attention on God and away from that which hinders you. Human beings constantly focus their attention on the rare problem cases, on lack, and not on the overwhelming abundance they experience all the time. The concept of the past serves to keep the attention on that, so you will not notice you are unlimited.

There are no problems. There are challenges to grow, to expand our consciousness. You are the designer of your challenges. Think about the divine instead of your problems. Bring everything which bothers you very much, all unpleasant experiences and fears into the light of God. God dissolves everything. By focusing your attention on your health, all physical complaints are healed. Think about that which functions correctly. If something surfaces about which you do not have positive thoughts, just remember a moment in the past in which your body functioned well in that respect. If that did not occur formerly, make an image in your mind of it and say to yourself: 'my body is very healthy, because—I can hear very well, see, smell, taste, eat, chew, lie down, sit, stand, breathe, think, etc. All my incorrect perceptions and thoughts about this body are now healed by God. For that is God's Will. I am whole and perfect in every respect. I am a divine creature. I have a divine body. This is how God views me. And God is always right.

I let go of every belief in lack. In Divine Reality no lack of any kind is possible. There is no lack of health or love or supply or life-time. I am Spirit. That is why I am always fresh and new and ageless. There is only abundant good, wholeness and perfect health.'

You are a spiritual being with a body consciousness. The body is just like all the material, an image in your mind. It serves as a means of communication and learning aid here. Your body's function is to enable your true self to experience the material world. For this it is perfect. That is why you can love the body. With this you can remind other parts of your Self who we are and thus remember who you are. You are meant to be whole, complete, perfect in this present moment. That is the purpose of the Almighty. There is no other will or law or power. That is why you cannot suffer lack. That is why your body is in reality perfect, in good shape, supple, flawless and thoroughly healthy, invulnerable and made to last forever. That is the way God willed it. You have a divine body. Perfection is your natural state. You are entitled to a perfectly healthy life, you only have to accept it. You are a device for Divine Spirit. You can be a channel for divine love and healing and miracles if you so choose.

There is no death, for that is not God's Will. Every experience of death and lack is a hallucination. Your body is a perfect, divine and spiritual idea in the One Mind. You live eternally, for the spirit in you is Divine and can never change. Your life is God's life; that is why you don't have to be afraid of uncertainty and change and death. That which you are is eternal and immortal and can never change. Time is only a medium to be able to experience another way of creating. Enjoy everything time offers you.

What does the perfect image God has of man, look like? Jesus has demonstrated this. Every image of ourselves that we manifest reflects what we believe about ourselves. And when we believe that we are the way God meant us to be, our body reflects the perfection which is our true inheritance. The lie of lack in any form is then forgotten. We know this is true, for every human being knows about an ideal of the body, however grotesque one may picture this ideal. The image of an ideal body is of course beyond the reach of the limited imagination, but let us remind ourselves that everything here is a distorted image of reality. The resurrection Jesus demonstrated was not only one of the soul, but also of the body. In his time on earth he healed all limited thoughts; every lack that was presented to him, he healed by only acknowledging the perfect. And death will be the last to overcome. We, who realize our oneness with God, know we can have no beginning and no end. We know our existence is spiritual and therefore unlimited and infinite.

By changing our mind we experience the manifestation of health and lasting prosperity. The belief in pain, suffering, sickness and death is driven out to make room for the certainty and expression of divine abilities God gave us; the realization we were always whole and perfect, for that is what comes forth from God.

We were never anything else. We could pretend we were limited and mortal, but we could not make it real. Innately we have inherited spirit from God. This is our heritage; we are just like God and therefore unchangeable and perfect. When we are convinced of this, it has to manifest in our bodies and our circumstances, for that is God's Will and what God wills, is done.

Forget everything the ego has taught you until now; it has only brought you pain. When Jesus said that we should be like little children, he was not only referring to their level of awareness of Self, but he also meant: open your mind to learn, realizing you know nothing and learn to let go of your destructive thoughts. And that is every thought you had till now. Doubtless that is a hard task, but we have divine help in our struggle. Our greatest stumbling block is if we think we know something and hold onto our silly opinions, judgments and insane 'sane' mind. You can readily assume, that every thought the untrained thinking has about anything, is foolish. Sometimes you think you already know the truth and have no idea how much more there is.

To get to know divine infinity we should open for more. As long as you see the smallest trace of mortal existence, the realm of the dead, the world of those who think they are alive, transformation is still needed.

In my experience this lesson was demonstrated to me by a woman who had lived in opulence all her life. In her transformation process she got rid of all her money, mainly because she gave it all away. She felt an inner urge to do this, without understanding what motivated her. This woman was like all mortals, very opiniated and had a lot of superstitious ideas. She felt that she knew everything already. No one could teach her anything. When her money was spent and she had to start making a living, the wall around her began to show some cracks. For the first time in her life she could truly consider something new and then the transformation of her thought-world really began. Now her life is filled with miracles.

When we set out on this path our lack of willingness to let our minds be changed is a very large stumbling block. The ego of people on this path often seems to be strongly developed. In fact that is logical; this is a path that demands great willpower. After the first infusion of light we can still be confronted with some of our worst trials. When we meet them in the right manner, they dissolve. If not, we surely will get another chance to choose again! You don't have to condemn yourself if you did not do the right thing immediately, for you are actually always innocent. You are a pupil and if you let the Holy Spirit guide you, you are totally innocent. You do have more responsibility, for after all, you now know more. But if you allow the Holy Spirit to lead you, you cannot suffer in any way.

It is certain that these trials advance the growth of our spiritual consciousness. Everything we accepted as true, shows up again, so we can look at it another time and choose again. In this way our mind is purified, till our consciousness is refilled with divine thoughts.

Within the frame of our learning process we are confronted automatically with our own convictions and belief in evil. The Bible gives a very graphic example of this in the tale of Job. He thought he was very spiritual and knew everything. Nevertheless he believed in evil and when he harvested the fruit of that and things went bad for him he accused God. It is difficult to believe we ourselves have chosen sickness, misery and death, but we could not be here if that was not so. The story of Job also illustrates that we maintain our misery by continuously repeating the story of loss and trouble. We must let go of the past. Stirring up the past is like digging up a corpse; both are illegal.

We are also confronted with opposition and attack. When we strive to raise the human consciousness we encounter seeming obstructions which we built in to stop us from denying this world. We had to or we could not have remained here and deny Reality. The ego is made to crucify the Christ, it is the anti-Christ. The ego tries to crucify everyone who acts out of real love. It is constantly upset and angry and feels everything as an attack. It is constantly looking around to see who is trying to rob it of its peace that it does not even have! It demands to be massaged and wants us to agree with it. But the ego has no power at all that we do not give it. That is why I no longer bend for insanity.

Moreover, through this opposition we find our certainty. Confronted with such counteraction we notice that our conviction is irrepressible. It is also delightful to notice how the divine love continues to flow in us and goes out to these so-called enemies. As long as your old conditioning is still active people can activate your feelings of unease. But regardless of your emotional reactions you perceive the flow of divine love. From this we can tell that emotional love is not love. Divine love is not just a feeling.

It may seem like a difficult path, but appearances deceive. All beginnings are hard. Every other path leads to pain, suffering and death. It is the only path to lasting peace, joy and freedom. What is truly difficult is denying Reality and forgetting who you are, thus living a lie. Yet we succeeded in doing that; will it not be much easier to let our memory return?

It appears as if we ask God to help us to sail around these stumbling blocks. We are really asking for help to be vigilant and for insight in the mechanisms of the ego, not through analysis, but through immediate, direct knowledge. As we understand the divine laws better, the circumstances in our lives improve. Our relationships are mainly harmonious, we enjoy radiant health and life's tribulations pass us by. We thank God and know that It is the only Source of good.

But if we are not vigilant the ego appropriates these achievements and instead of thinking 'I am better of than before' the thought comes up; 'I am better than others because God goes with me'. It sounds absurd, but pride in spiritual achievements exists. Consequently you are tempted to demonstrate how much spiritual power you have. It is also possible that it becomes some sort of measure of the spiritual status. The ego is proud of all the wrong things, the temporary and transitory. It is not proud of you! You are the Christ, the divine spirit expressing in form. We try to appear little in order not to threaten the lack in self-esteem in the other, as Oprah Winfrey once remarked in her talk-show.

The Christ does not have a superiority complex. He is superior to anything unreal, but He makes no comparison. That would indeed be futile. He sees only himself, everywhere He looks. But he is also not burdened by false humility. It is not arrogant to be your true Self. It is only arrogant to pretend to be something that you're not.

Another temptation is growing willfulness. When we discover it is possible to claim everything, we can be tempted to decide our own course. We see that happening with people who indulge themselves sexually. When even the slightest bit of light has come everything comes within our reach. That is why it is necessary for your thinking to be purified first, for you obtain unimaginable power. Every possibly harmful thought has to be removed from your mind. The power to perform miracles cannot rest in those who could harm. Not because they are evil, but because they still live in illusion.

However, it is possible to have everything. All the material can flow abundantly in our experience. Money can do strange things with us, though. But the self-imposed limitation of strict poverty is no different. God does not want to limit us in any way. It is possible that things, relationships and chaotic urges, which would interfere with our transformation, vanish from our world of experience. But that only happens because your inner guidance prevents you as much as possible from hurting yourself any longer and therefore helps you to find your true Self by the shortest way.

The temptation is attachment to earthly pleasure and earthly goods, not the experience or possession of them. You are then attached to the possession of dust and that is the possession of nothing. It is helpful to ask yourself what you want possessions for; if you really need them, they will in a natural way come abundantly to you. If you think they will bring you joy, realize you don't know what will make you happy. God knows. On the spiritual path the issue is not advancement of your material circumstances, for that happens naturally. As you release your limited thoughts, you also release your belief in material limitations.

When we truly live in abundance, we focus on what we can give, not on what we can get. Often people don't know what they want. That is a very good starting point. For you really don't know what is right for you. You can then ask for the revelation of your Will. You could also ask; 'Divine Self, reveal my vocation—what would you have me do?'

And so you discover the Will of God for you. Don't be surprised if suddenly all kinds of information about your inner powers and about God surfaces. These data show you the answer to your question. For knowledge of your divine essence makes you happy.

If people think they know what they want they have no vision whether that would really make them happy. For one need has hardly been satisfied or the other surfaces. They have lost the ability to discern pain from pleasure. Things that bring us joy, do that very briefly and do not bring harmony to all involved. If we think a partner will make us happy, because we don't want to be alone (as if that could be possible!), we will find someone to fill that need. But as soon as that is done we notice other needs, which we translate in demands on the other. We behave as if we are here to manipulate and dominate others. You try to coerce others to do what you think you want, but your very resistance makes them give you the experience of that which you do not want. Thus we remain in conflict, the experience of lack and limitation.

Mortal happiness is temporary. The car or the relationship or improved health or that particular job or promotion will not make you eternally happy. This is no argument in favor of poverty or lack; on the spiritual path attachment to this also poses a temptation. Orthodox Christians used to equate detachment with deprivation. That is not God's Will.

There are not two worlds, the world of God and the world of humans. There is only one reality and whoever does not see it, lives in a hallucination. The spiritual principles are applicable in every day's routine. If we do not see the desired result immediately in our lives, however, let us not make the hallucination real. One just has to keep on keeping on and be patient. Learning a totally different way of life does not happen in a day. Even without material rewards like improved health or prosperity a new world has emerged for those on this path. The gradual unfoldment of Truth offers a view on delightful new possibilities and wonderful experiences. Transcending dualism and realization of oneness with God ushers us into a completely new world. And for some time we abide in some kind of borderland, in which the old is gone, but the new has not yet presented itself. It is very tempting to halt at the material miracles, at the improvement of your earthly circumstances. But your kingdom is not of this world.

A large stumbling block is formed by attachment, wanting to cling to an experience and repeat it over and over again. Not desire is the root of evil, it is the desire to cling, the desire for repetition. That is always motivated by fear. You don't agree with what you have and experience lack. It has been said before that this is a wrong perspective. Jesus did not encourage us to conquer desire, but to focus it on God. You are that which experiences, which has to experience. You are the witness of God. That is what desire is for. However, it is used by your limited I to keep you out of the present experience, the now. If you are constantly preoccupied with fearful and painful things from the past and asking for another future, you are not completely in the experience of the now.

In many thought schools it is believed that desire causes suffering. No teacher has ever succeeded in saving man from desire, though, because it comes from God. The teacher has only learned to focus the desire in him correctly, so the emptiness in him could be filled. He may think then that he has overcome every desire. Deep inside we know that it is right to long for love, peace, safety, abundance and joy. We also long for acknowledgement, but that is again an ego version of the desire to let the divine light shine through us, to know our self-worth. We know we are entitled to all these things, for they were given us by God. If a teacher has found peace and preaches that we should let go of every desire, he obviously does not recognize the way the process works. We cannot really know why spiritual teachers make such statements or if they even do, because the teachings have often been presented falsely.

However, Jesus provided us with the insight that we don't have to tear desire from our hearts. We only have to direct it consciously toward God. Joel Goldsmith told us to answer any thought of lack with the realization: 'God's mercy is sufficient for me. I need nothing else.' (2 Cor.12:9)

Does the desire to do evil come from God then? Gardner Hunting wrote about this in 'Working with God':

'But you remind me that I have said that all desire comes from God. It may be well enough to think that the desire to work comes from the one power, but does the desire of the thief to steal come also from the Supreme Being? To steal, no. To possess, yes. Every instinct, appetite and aspiration is implanted in man by God. But who is God? Why, God is my Creator. God is my life, my strength, my intelligence, my mind. Now turn the statement around. My being is God, my life is God, my intelligence is God, my

mind is God. Do you pretend to say that you have a desire independent of your mind? Hardly. Well, that is the answer.'

The ego also abuses the longing for enlightenment. The seeker does not know what he is really looking for. Nevertheless, it is not right to accuse seekers of egoism. You can be mistaken in your identity, but you can never be too preoccupied with the question: 'Who am I?' Everyone is fascinated by this question. It is constantly asked in human consciousness and the ego answers with different diversion tactics and condemnations, which have less and less effect. God Himself has placed the question there, because it is the Will of God that you redis-cover who you are.

Even though the longing for God implies a lack, it is the only per-ceived lack that is not answered with the experience of more lack. You can deduce from that that longing was made so we could experience the infinity of God. For every longing is essentially longing for God.

When we have found God, we experience a state in which we have no desires left. That is the peace which surpasses every human under-standing. There is inner silence and a stirring emptiness, which is inde-scribable.

Whatever you are experiencing now, it is of your own making. If that is lack, you must have thought it necessary on some level, or you would not have asked for that experience. The ego rejoices when you experience lack. I remember very distinctly the approval and sympathy I received when I shared my 'problems' with other. We didn't know better, we were accustomed to join in suffering. The more miserable our story was, the more interesting we appeared to be for others.

However, you can desire without experiencing lack. You could see desire as placing an order. It then becomes more a kind of anticipation. It is not complete desirelessness, but since little importance is attached to the outcome and the desire is not based on a feeling of lack, you could rather characterize it as a feeling of glad anticipation, in which there is the conviction that whatever happens, all is well. One just has a slight preference as to the experience one wishes to have in consciousness. We don't lose sight of the fact that only God knows what is truly in our own best interest and serves our relationship with Him and that that comes first.

For the ego it is a bitter perspective that one only will enjoy lasting prosperity and other fruits when there is no attachment left. For this is a feeling of lack and that leads to the experience of more lack. As long as we do not let go of any desire to better our human situation, that desire maintains the situation. We then are in the experience of lack. It is not the desire for more happiness, that causes suffering. It is the experience of lack of happiness, that is responsible for our suffering. But by redirecting our attention on Reality, this grows in our awareness.

The difference people make between an inner and an outer world is not real. Everything is in your consciousness, in your inner world. The so-called outer world also. You can experience something else than the dualistic world by focusing your attention on something else. Whatever you let the light of your attention shine on, will be increased in your experience. If you let your light shine on illusions, that is what you will experience. Focus your attention on the kingdom of God and that will appear to you. We find out that what we considered weak at first turns out to be the greatest force in the universe. Let us seek the kingdom of God. Then we will be saved from every belief in lack and we will see that everything has already been given us.

Claim your true inheritance, the divine peace and joy that are eternal, that are the core of your being. The rest will follow. Once the manifestation of spiritual riches and health was rejected because it would not be 'spiritual'. Don't look down on it. God wants us to experience abundance in every respect. Everything we realize inwardly, will also manifest outwardly, unless we reject this.

God is power to create. We cannot create God, but we are the Christ and can create. Though the term 'expand' is more appropriate. 'Creation' presumes that something could be made that has a beginning and is done within a timeframe. Something that can be made, that has not always existed, cannot be permanent. Something that has a beginning, must also have an end.

To really extend, in stead of making the perishable, we first have to seek the kingdom of God, meaning we first have to become aware of our oneness and allow the Whole Spirit to lead us. All powers of the universe are directed towards this raising of consciousness, this awakening. That is why Divine Inspiration is available for everyone, either as intuition, or as a still small voice, our inner guidance. Seeking the kingdom 'first' does not entail a time sequencing. It means we have to put peace, love, oneness and harmony first in everything we want and do.

We ask God to deliver us from evil. We can keep on asking to be delivered from one setback after another, from the same recurring problems, but that is no real deliverance. We have to be delivered from the hell of dual thinking, our faith in evil, our faith in another power and another will than God's. For evil is the judging, the distinction we make between Self and not-self. Evil is faith in the power of evil, in lack of health, lack of love and companionship, lack of means to maintain the physical life. All the apparent evil we seem to perceive is not from God, it does not belong to the kingdom of God. Can there be anything outside of God, Who is everything?

We ask to be delivered from our belief in limitation, pain and suffering, vulnerability, sickness, old age and mortality, from our identification with a limited self and our fearful attachment to it. Ask yourself what the world would be like if everyone only believed in good and 'did not resist evil', in other words only focused the attention on the good?

It is not possible that there would be lack of the divine for us. There is no lack of love, health, prosperity, safety, agelessness and eternal life. The awareness of this is resurrected every holy instant. You are the power in your life. Your word is the law unto time, the weather, your financial situation, your body, your insight and knowledge, all your desires.

All power has been given unto you, all power is in your mind. Because our body expresses how we see ourselves, our body also is resurrected, it partakes in the renewal of our thinking. We then know: 'I only have the age of God, for God is my life. I live forever. I am timeless and ageless. My life cannot be limited in any way, despite the testimony of my senses. They are made to see illusions. The divine power is my immortal body, my health and vitality and beauty. God is immortality, health, vitality and beauty and is manifesting in this body.'

From our new perspective we see the body more and more as the perfect spiritual idea it is. All our material circumstances are part of this, they reflect our divine awakening. Awakening is raising of consciousness. That is what the resurrection of Jesus expresses. We have viewed it as an event that happened only once in the past, but that was not the message he wanted to convey. Jesus made it clear through the resurrection that we are immortal. It is not the incorrect body-image we have that lives forever, but our correct body-consciousness. We don't have to crucify ourselves any longer. We don't have to die any longer.

As the leader of the Endeavor Academy so eloquently put it:

'There is no death. Death is in your mind. By your retention of the necessity to exist (meaning; as a human being) you are dead. But there is no death. You have a desperate determination to undergo an experience of obliviation in order to justify yourself.'

He furthermore says:

'If you relinquish death you'll see that there's no purpose. If there is no death, why are you in a body, getting sick and dying? See how much you love death? How much you depend on it? How much you attack this message? You have to attack it. Why? There is no death. This is beyond belief.

The quicker you can look at 'you're the cause of this' the quicker you'll get out of here. If there really is no death, why do you stay here and die?

Now do you see why you need a miracle?'

Death is the last illusion we overcome. The companion we have relied on all our lives, turns out to be a shadowy phantom, a phantasm without any power. Everything that is not in God, is dead. It does not exist in Reality, it is playing in the no-thing. It presents itself for transformation. We look at all the forms of death we had made up and that present themselves to us, one after another, all our old thoughts that we projected outside of the image we had of ourselves. Everything that has pushed our 'buttons', that has hurt us, comes by one more time for a renewed evaluation to be made whole. Maybe for a moment we can feel the pain of them again. We don't defend ourselves, though, but we remain defenselessness, willing to be completely crushed by that which we have placed outside of ourselves. We look at them fearlessly and we turn them over to the light of the Divine Spirit, in which they dissolve forever. We don't resist anything, for we realize we must have asked for it (sometime). Moreover, it is a lot easier to go with the flow. We realize that the current moment is exactly as it should be. When we surrender to our circumstances and accept everything, we in fact become observers of the life of the personality we depict. We become disengaged from the results. In fact we consider every situation as an opportunity to raise our consciousness. We realize that all events come to us in our best interest, whatever they may look like, for we realize we are living in Gods universe, where evil does not exist. We affirm that the moment is exactly the way it should be. Why would you fight phantasms? We don't acquiesce, for we do not accept lies. If the events do not bring us peace, we can learn how to ask for peace. By acceptance and realization of our oneness with God we become aware again of our True Nature and our creative power. We know that God is present and that God wants the good for us. For in reality there is nothing else.

Our Lord, Jesus, taught us about the power of defenselessness. He said: 'If someone forces you to go one mile, also go the second mile with him.' (Matth.5:41) Who really has the power, when we do this? And as Taniguchi observed, this saying also illustrates the principle of infinite supply, that giving is receiving.

And as we realize that unlimited physical perfection is our reality, we wonder what happens to those who lay down their mortal bodies. Will those whose consciousness has resurrected, live eternally in material reality? In 'Dialogue on Awakening' by Tom Carpenter it is explained that death is like entering another room. You immediately want to return to the previous one.

That is why we will only leave the dimension of form completely when we have mastered our mind. As long as you appear here in form you apparently still have something to do here. The form does not only refer to the body you associate with. Finally you will take the body into the light by the process of Resurrection and operate from a dimension of higher frequency, as our Master, Jesus, has. Until then we learn to control the physical world of experiences again and to project bodies that radiate health.

So we remember that there are stumbling blocks, in order to watch out for them and take them to the light. Every suffering, even every so-called small disturbance of our peace of mind, a frown, is a temptation. There is something then we don't agree with, something in our nightmare that we make real. Faith in lack and evil. We cannot avoid this happening, as long as this world is in our consciousness. It has been pointed out that there are not two worlds, even though our senses try to convince us of the opposite. There is only one world. We are tempted to think that the world of the senses is real. But there is only the divine world. Whenever we see something that does not belong to the divine world we remind ourselves that God is here and now and is always available and that these appearances are not real. This is how we are freed from our delusions. It will not be transformed by suppressing it or merely deny it. Not by trying to change our external circumstances. That is just another diversion of the ego. We can transform it by facing it and asking for divine help. You change the world by changing your thoughts about it. The power of God in us then helps us to forgive and let go.

On the way to the house of our consciousness we have to let all beliefs be transformed. That is what we continually do, until we live in a world in which we only see God. As long as you are here, you are letting your old thoughts be transformed. Everything there is now in your consciousness, is a thought from the past. Thoughts you have projected and that have to be removed to make room for the new, for divine thoughts. By your vigilance you have placed yourself above the battleground, where you can watch those thoughts. You are no longer engaged in the drama and no longer live reactively. You realize that there is no one outside of you. No one who does anything to you and also no one who can change your mind for you, who can save you from yourself.

Until you see that you are doing it to yourself, that you have made everything up and realize that you don't have to do this anymore. Then you see: I thought there was a power that depressed me. Maybe there was a chemical imbalance in my body or something that I have no control over. However, that is not the case. It is a thought about yourself. It is part of your identity. You decide how to react. When it is winter, I am depressed, in fall I have the flu, if I don't get a promotion, I am discontented. It is all made up. You are nothing you can define.

But to remove the old thoughts you need divine help, for you cannot do that yourself.

8

Asking God to deliver us from our evil thoughts.

Asking to be delivered from evil is a request for God's Presence, for through this we are delivered from the evil in our thought-world. That is also the only place any evil can be. God knows nothing of evil and sin, or He would be a sinful God. It would then be in Him. He would be it. Where God is, no thought of another power can enter.

We should recognize no other power and bend in no way to any other power. Not only the power we attributed to talismans and other magical symbols is meant, but every belief in an evil power, a power outside of us. Let it be clear, that the earth has been given to Satan, but Satan is not a creature! Satan is and always has been a lie. 'A lie from the beginning' the Bible calls it. The earth is ruled by a lie, the belief in the lie of the power of evil, that is symbolically referred to as Satan.

God is the only real power and the only evil we can be delivered from is the evil we have made up, our delusions.

We are several gradations, forms of the one Consciousness, awakening together to the perfection of the whole of the Christ-consciousness. Consciousness experiences what is in it. Through that the human actually lives in different worlds. In fact we are always conscious and connected. Only in our human perception a separation has occurred. It seems to be losing its grip on us and that the whole world is waking up. It looks as if all of us are becoming aware of our divine abilities and our lives in divine reality. In all of us there is divine light and love, peace and joy and Truth and our consciousness of that is apparently increasing. But in fact all of us are already home and merely observing the impossibility of that which never happened.

This is how we regain the faith in our immortality, our timelessness. Spirit cannot die. The images in the mind can change, the movie you are watching can change, but you do not change. The ego is afraid of loss of identity. But the I you feel is you, is God's remembrance of you. God always sees you as an individual, perfect and whole, a unique expression of Him.

You always remain the same. Thinking your real Self is outside of your normal consciousness is a belief that limits your self-expression. When we all have become conscious, we will create a completely different world. All our senseless ideas about 'laws of nature' will dissolve and we will see the new earth that was always there. First the slate of the mind has to be wiped clean, purified of all misunderstandings, before you can understand this. Darkness seems real until the light begins to shine. Then it becomes clear that darkness is not something, not a being, but merely the absence of light. This is what happens to every belief in mortal laws when the light of the Divine Spirit shines in the consciousness of someone. You can view the world as a cult, that has brainwashed you. You need to be deprogrammed. Limitation is an experience, but there is a Reality in which limitation is not real. There you can experience inner peace. Christ gives a peace that is completely different from that of the world. What the world gives is very fleeting. It is more like a temporary feeling of satiation, a temporary absence of discontent. The peace that surpasses all human understanding can be felt everywhere and always, under all circumstances.

When the light has come we see that every suffering is unnecessary. We would like to save everyone immediately. There is then the trap of glorifying the ego, for we can start gathering followers who place us on a pedestal. A precarious position, as history teaches us. Our Lord Jesus said: 'Why do you call me good?' He also said: 'From myself I can do nothing.' We should only call God good. All the good we express is a manifestation of God. Before we plunge on our neighbor to deliver him, we should allow the Holy Inspiration to purify our thinking, for transcending our human conditioning may take a while. It is useless to try to release others from their suffering with an untrained mind. You don't have to know everything, because the Holy Inspiration will guide you, but first you need to be trained let Him lead the way. There is always the temptation to assert your own will and dominate others. But even if you have the best intentions, and you are only trying to convince them, every forced change you bring about, is only temporary. God does the work in people. The Holy Spirit will let you know when you are ready for this. That is much sooner then you think. Be glad with every quiet day, for that is the silence before the storm. Once your service starts, continual endeavor is demanded. When you're ready, this service is happily given.

We have already discussed the temptation of attachment to physical pleasure, material things or on the contrary, denying yourself things. There is also the temptation to let go of further effort in consciousness raising, once people experience the miracle of health or prosperity.

We can also tend to continue to trust in human means and lies. Even Peter, who had witnessed so many miracles, denied Jesus, because he feared for his freedom and his life. We then do not give our fear to the Holy Spirit, but try to cope with the effects with lies. When Peter said 'I don't know him', he actually said he didn't know God. Judas sold his spiritual heritage and we can only speculate about his motivation. When we stand still on our journey home because we have already received more than we had ever thought possible, we are in fact doing the same thing.

There is also the temptation to flee from your brothers. Especially in the beginning stages of our awakening it is difficult to cope with the attacks of the ego. For a while we have to hide the Christ in 'Egypt'. But you are not supposed to stay in hiding. Nor is it possible.

Being around someone who consistently views things differently demands much from both parties. The awakened person can no longer share the view of the unhealed mind. The realization that they are your own unhealed thoughts, depicted for you, doesn't really make it easier. The ego doesn't surrender so easily. It labels anyone who continually disagrees, be it silent or aloud, as loveless. People are so used to unite in grievances and pain and opinions, that they consider someone who doesn't join with them in suffering as 'loveless'. Loving to them is sharing each other's suffering and affirming each other's limitations. We often feel a certain unity by sharing our complaints and grievances and judgments. The feeling it gives is like a faint shadow of the true unity, we so desperately long for and that was never lost. It is sad and ridiculous. When someone does not agree with us, that feels like an attack. You cannot bring the two thought-systems in agreement.

The person who is not aware and feels the attraction of the light, often has his own ideas about the way the awakening should take place, how the teachers on the path to consciousness raising should proceed. It should be done 'lovingly', which for the sleeper means 'please let me sleep'.

Acting lovingly means that human ideas are no longer permitted to rule the earthly existence. Isn't it more loving to risk one's neck and show people the way out? Some leaders of major mystery-schools claim that this is not for the masses. That those who reveal the secrets will be nailed to the cross of public opinion. Another delusional idea in the human thought-world, that we no longer should believe. Jesus has already died on the cross and demonstrated there is no 'death'. We don't have to crucify each other and ourselves anymore. When we seem to be attacked for speaking the Truth, let us not feel hurt.

As soon as we have been touched by God we want to share our treasure with everyone. We are upset when others are not as happy with it as we are. They don't know the experience and try to put it down. You can feel worthless then, because your thinking is trained insufficiently to handle these attacks in the right way.

Everyone who listens to the voice of the Holy Inspiration experiences that the world considers it an attack when you don't agree with its dreams. If you don't join in complaining or express pity for others, that is seen as loveless. The ego looks for allies, people who prove them right in their imaginary conflicts.

When you are angry, you try to get rid of the pain by giving it to another. You cannot get rid of it that way. It always ends in more pain, for you as well. You are in fear and don't realize your worth. The unreal you lacks self-worth and has a limited self-image. In fact you feel worthless, unloved and unsafe. You choose attack to avoid facing those feelings. You fear Truth more than anything and prefer empty ego-massage.

Humans don't know what love is. Supporting insane thoughts of people who think that the good, God, lacks in their life, who have judge everything and see evil and lack everywhere, is not love. Love is to point out that their sense of separation is ridiculous, that they cannot lack anything and are one with everything. That they are always receiving everything they have asked for. God so loves them that they even receive the impossible, namely the mortal experience.

If people condemn you when you live in the Christ-consciousness, that means you are on the right way. Jesus says that you are blessed, when you are slandered and persecuted for his sake. Rejoice, for your reward is great in heaven, for likewise they also persecuted the prophets before you.

Nothing scares the ego more then the Christ. But do not be mistaken: It is also possible that criticism is directed at you because of your incorrect attitude. Sometimes one thinks he is persecuted because of this faith, but he is rejected because he rejects others first, who do not have the same faith, by seeing them as sinners who are condemned to hell and other misery. And considering himself therefore as better. It is also possible that the criticism reflects an anticipation in you that you will be criticized or it reflects your suppressed criticism. Maybe you do not approve of yourself or you still find parts of the Truth offensive. People often fear the reaction of others to the insight that the world isn't real, until it has become an irrefutable experience.

Criticism also is valuable. Through opposition you find your certainty. Be grateful for your critics, for your faith is then tested and you discover whether and how certain you are.

Those who live in the Christ-consciousness, do not think of themselves as better than others, but they do see themselves as better of than formerly. That is not a personal merit, that is mercy and you would wish that for everyone. You would like to give that to everyone, it is not something you want to keep to yourself. However, you can only bring the light and healing where it is welcome, where it no longer causes fear.

The ego can only exist if we deny our oneness. When the light has come, it is not possible anymore to rub ego's. Your incorrect self-image would then be confirmed and this would prolong the suffering. The ego would like to claim divinity and immortality, though. But that is impossible, and it knows that, and that's another reason for it to feel rejected.

The human existence is like a depiction of the separation from God. Let us release this idea and accept our oneness with each other and with God. Jesus said: 'Go and sin no more. He meant: Don't be separate from God any longer.

We must not isolate ourselves from our brothers who are dreaming. In the Bible it is pointed out that if a man cannot love his brother, who he has seen, how will he then love God, who he has not seen? Only by perceiving the divine in the other, we can begin to perceive it in ourselves. We have to see the Divine Spirit in our neighbor, even if his behavior reflects the most horrible characteristics. Fortunately we can ask our inner teacher for help with this. We don't have to go looking for the true essence of our brother. We only have to be willing to see it and not to blame him for his nightmares. And persist in this willingness, despite that which our senses tell us about the other. In every child of God there is a spiritual essence. Let us find the love to be willing to see that and only that. For only when we see mankind with the eyes of God will we see our true origin.

Seeing the suffering of humanity the thought surfaces to help them. But remember, every soul is entitled to its own experiences. If God Himself does not interfere, who are we to determine what the soul of another needs? However, God does not want us to remain in hell. Those who are able to accept our help will be led to us by the Holy Spirit as soon as we have become a usable instrument. We must keep in mind that we should not join with another in misery, but in love and joy. We can only help by remaining above the troubles. You cannot help someone who is going down in quicksand by jumping in too. When you worry, you only make the situation worse. We can help by realizing that God is working in and for that person. And that it isn't real. The one we see 'suffering' is a holy child of God, just like God and cannot suffer.

Whatever is suffering is not real. It is a wrong identification. Because of that it is make believe, it is a role. Recognize that that soul has assumed that role for you. If you see anyone who is angry or suffering from other expressions of lack, you should be grateful to that person for playing that role for you. Pure love motivates them to enable you to experience the impossible, namely limitation. You then help in the realization that you are here to save your world. Not to join in an old nightmare. On the contrary, the goal is to awaken those aspects of your Self, that are still living in that nightmare. In every contact with your neighbors your aim is then to speak the Word of God and to be a vessel for the Christ. That is why you give them the Love of God. That also includes not participating in any of their dreams. They are allowed to participate in yours, because that is a dream of awakening. Little by little you will notice that they do that with total dedication. For they have agreed with you to depict in time every conviction you have.

For those among us who are just beginning to experience their power, there is the realistic danger of abuse of power to satisfy needs of the ego. The need for power is legitimate, for you are a powerful being and you want to remember that. But seeking power outside of you through sexual or psychological domination or manipulation or through abuse of worldly goods and position will never fulfill you, for it is external power and therefore temporal. You then strangle creation in stead of allowing it to lie down at your feet in total joyful surrender to itself. The ego translates your divine desire in a desire for more money, worldly power, fame. How can you cope with this?

Let us first consider sexual excesses. Who is the boss—God or your sexual organs? Many teachers end up in this trap. Every form of sex is based in fact on the misguided idea that uniting bodies can be a substitute for our divine union. In the ego-world this idea is not popular, that is why enlightenment is as difficult for the ego as it is for a camel to go through the eye of a needle. For ego it is impossible and for the enlightened nothing is easier. He does not see anything that is attractive in any body. He does not merely exchange his energy during intercourse, but on every level. But you don't have to condemn yourself if you are still in the experience of primitive sexual desire. It is the desire for our original oneness. In everything we do, we are seeking God. Only, we won't find God by uniting bodies. When we experience the oneness with God, we transcend sexual desire gradually. Unless we don't want to and attach great value to sex. By realizing oneness with God we obtain true oneness with everything and everyone and inner peace. Then the search for something outside of us is over. We then begin our inner journey of discovery and are delighted by the revelation of every aspect of our true Self. Our body energies then are also directed differently.

Isn't tantra a road to enlightenment then? Every conscious union with God leads us into the oneness. Our goal is contact with our Divine Self. Sexuality can be used to reach God, just like dishwashing, to raise our consciousness. It is a technique of meditation during or involving sexual intimacy. You can ask yourself why it would have to be done in such a complicated way, while you can easily sit down and connect to the divine thought world. Meditation does not become more attractive or easier by associating it with sex. It can very easily become another diversion tactic. The school from which tantra has emerged has mapped flows of energy and phenomena accompanying transformation, however. For many seekers who were confronted with all sorts of unexpected and unfamiliar energetic sensations this knowledge is indispensable. The Holy Spirit really uses everything for good.

The temptations are strongest, when one decides to leave them behind. In the following text James Allen provides us with insight concerning that.

'Immediately the resolution to walk a higher path is made, temptation and trial begin. Men have found that no sooner have they decided to lead a truer and nobler life than they have been overwhelmed with such a torrent of new temptations and difficulties as make their position almost unendurable, and many men, because of this, relinquish their resolution.

But these temptations and trials are a necessary part of the work of regeneration upon which the man has decided and must be hailed as friends and met with courage if the resolution is to do its work. For what is the real nature of a resolution? Is it not the sudden checking of a particular stream of conduct, and the endeavour to open up an entirely new channel? Think of an engineer who decides to turn the course of a powerfully running stream or river in another direction. He must first cut his new channel, and must take every precaution to avoid failure in the carrying out of his undertaking. But when he comes to the all-important task of directing the stream into its new channel, then the flowing force, which for ages has steadily pursued its accustomed course, becomes refractory, and all the patience and care and skill of the engineer will be required for the successful completion of the work. It is even so with the man who determines to turn his course of conduct in another and higher direction. Having prepared his mind, which is the cutting of a new channel, he then proceeds to the work of redirecting his mental forces—which have hitherto flowed on uninterruptedly—into the new course. Immediately this is attempted, the arrested energy begins to assert itself in the form of powerful temptations and trials hitherto unknown and unencountered. And this is exactly as it should be; it is the law; and the same law that is in the water is in the mind. No man can improve upon the established law of things, but he can learn to under-

stand the law instead of complaining, and wishing things were different. The man who understands all that is involved in the regeneration of his mind will 'glory in tribulations,' knowing that only by passing through them can he gain strength, obtain purity of heart, and arrive at peace.'

Sexuality was not made by God, despite the sex gurus who are preaching that. You can have everything, but that does not mean that it is divine. Sex is nothing. The fleeting nature of sexual pleasure also demonstrates that. We cannot unite physically, only spiritually. That spiritual union can be felt as an energetic experience. The divine union leads to permanent oneness, peace and bliss. The peace sex gives is only temporary satisfaction. The ego does not agree with this, because it cannot imagine the continual experience of oneness. It then feels attacked and condemned and lashes out. For it considers sexuality as an indispensable weapon to control you. Do not let the ego dictate how you should feel. You also don't have to take my word for it or Jesus'. You only have to enter the silence and constantly ask your inner teacher for the Truth and investigate how you feel. If your life is filled with sexual pleasure, are you happy? Do you feel good about yourself? Do you have lasting inner peace? Or are you looking for fulfillment in another? Do you treat others as you would like to be treated? Do you identify them with a body or do you see the divine Spirit in them? Ask yourself what you want this for. And then just ask for what you want. You do everything to find happiness and peace. You are willing to do the most awful things for that. Humans are not addicted to anything, they are just looking for God in the wrong things. They think anesthesia, the suppression of pain, is happiness.

Uncontrolled sexual behavior is often seen as an addiction. But in fact they are addicted to a temporary feeling of power. A feeling that reminds you for a moment who you really are.

Let go of every feeling of guilt, also those about sexual behavior. If God Himself does not condemn you, why would you? The guilty cannot learn. You are innocent, because you are ignorant. At the same time you are responsible, because only you can change something. You can unlearn old habits and in that process you can still make mistakes. That is why you need divine help. As long as you are here, you are still learning. When you are completely identified with the Christ, you definitely won't be here anymore.

Power always intoxicates the ego. When you receive recognition, the ego can take possession of it. We all know what a bloated ego is capable of.

When we see a brother, who does not serve Love in Christ-consciousness and tries to use his worldly power to dominate and manipulate others, we can ask if we want to hold onto this image or surrender it to the Light. For there is no person. There is only the Christ and a hallucination, the ego, a thought-system that we are working out and viewing together. At the most there is an actor, playing that role. He deserves our love and encouragement to lay down that role. We have asked him to play that insane role. Every thought of attack is collective.

The stumbling blocks that greed, and desire for recognition form are clearly demonstrated in our time by the power struggle that has followed the words of Jesus in 'Jesus' Course in Miracles'. A mind filled with plans for attack anticipates attack everywhere and is engaged in defense. Just as there was an attempt to distort the original teaching of the Master (and that seemed to succeed for almost 2000 years) people are now posing as 'defenders' of the integrity of the words of Jesus. They employ all worldly means of power the ego has made up. The ego is so insane that it thinks it can act as protector of the Light. We immediately know then that the ego is active, because the Light does not need defense. The ego longs for money, power and to surround itself with obedient followers.

The same people who pretend to defend the words of Jesus, claim that Christianity has nothing in common with the Course. One even said that the gospel is something else than what Jesus himself has transmitted to one of his channels, Helen Shucman. In a court case they are persecuting others in order to defend a copyright they claim to have to the words of Jesus.

During the court case the solicitors even claimed that the Jesus of the Course is not the same as the Jesus from the gospels.

So history repeats itself. The ego has tried from the start to distort the teaching of Jesus. First it was contaminated with Manicheism, undiluted dualism posing as religion. Now others are trying to contaminate the Truth again. Many would have liked to correct them, but were afraid to, out of fear of appearing publicly as that which they abhor. But it is attack if we leave an unhealed thought in darkness. We should look at that which the current situation around the teaching of Jesus represents in our thought world and let the light of Truth shine on it. Jesus says 'forgive and this will disappear…' We can ask for correction of this image of attack in our minds.

These associations have taken it upon them to demonstrate how temptation in the form of longing for external power can work out. Our temptation would be to make it real and not see the Divine spark in them anymore. We ask the Holy Spirit to make them conscious, to help them to awaken and to give up their plans for attack on the plan for salvation. They no longer have to crucify the Christ for us. They don't have to depict this anymore. Let them express their authentic, true Self. That is what we love and that is what we want to see. You must have attacked the Light somehow sometime, or you wouldn't be able to see this. Let us not condemn another for his fear-based thoughts. He deserves Truth and Love. There is only one pain, only one dream. Join the dreamer, not the dream.

Keep his reality in mind. Nothing can stop the Will of God and it is Gods Will that your brother also awakens on the appointed time. You will experience that. Leave him to God.

The ego cannot win. Light dispels darkness. Darkness is dispelled by contact with the very thing it wants to destroy. The ego can only procrastinate and thus evade the inevitable for a while. But ultimately you will put a stop to it through the purification of your mind.

The familiar arguments are also discussed by James Allen.

'We have heard it said that reason is a blind guide, and that it draws men away from Truth rather than leads them to it. If this were true, it were better to remain, or to become, unreasonable, and to persuade others so to do. We have found, however, that the diligent cultivation of the divine faculty of reason brings about calmness and mental poise, and enables one to meet cheerfully the problems and difficulties of life.

It is true there is a higher light than reason; even that of the Spirit of Truth itself, but without the aid of reason, Truth cannot be apprehended. They who refuse to trim the lamp of reason will never, whilst they so refuse, perceive the light of Truth, for the light of reason is a reflection of that Light.'

He continues to argue that people who think they can approach Truth merely emotionally, are mistaken.

'For reason leads away from passion and selfishness into the quiet ways of sweet persuasion and gentle forgiveness, and he will never be led astray, nor will he follow blind guides, who faithfully adheres to the Apostolic injunction, 'Prove all things, and hold fast that which is good.' They, therefore, who despise the light of reason, despise the Light of Truth.

Large numbers of people are possessed of the strange delusion that reason is somehow intimately connected with the denial of the existence of God. This is probably due to the fact that those who try to prove that there is no God usually profess to take their stand upon reason, while those who try to prove the reverse generally profess to take their stand on faith. Such argumentative combatants, however, are frequently governed more by prejudice than either reason or faith, their object being not to find Truth, but to defend and confirm a preconceived opinion.

Most people are constantly struggling with their circumstances, trying to change them. They are then trying to change the symptoms. That which they experience can only change permanently if they change the cause, their own belief system. There is only one way to have lasting prosperity, truly warm relationships, freedom in every way, happiness, beauty, purpose, love, peace and joy in your life. That is by letting your thoughts be changed. If you really want those things, you can have them. You only have to unlearn to accept the thought world of limitation, of the ego, as yours. You only have to learn to think again.

H. Emilie Cady already posed the question in 'Lessons in Truth':

'If all thinking is God, how could we then have wrong thoughts or think something else then God's thoughts?'

There is only one Mind, and in that world of experiences a simulation, a game of make believe is executed. That game is clearly based on the idea of a world without God. That is why there is a religious doctrine that 'this world was given to Satan'. It has been pointed out before, however, that this so-called evil is not real, it is a lie, a play. The individual intellect is the tool of this simulation. Based on the fundamental assumption that good and evil exist, through our reasoning ability, analyzing, labeling, evaluating, and judging we can experience a dual reality. You can liken the human perception to a narrowed vision. Since there can be no separation from Spirit, the human world of experiences, however limited, is also part of that. It is just another way of being. The mortal thinking, that thinks in opposites, is mainly based on that which appears as the outside world, the so-called objective material reality. Humans believe that this so-called reality is not connected to their beliefs about it. They believe that they can merely trace the laws it obeys. But this assumption is completely incorrect, like all others in mortal thinking. Emilie Cady cites Paul who says in Romans 8:6: 'the mind of the flesh is death; but the mind of the Spirit is life and peace.' She explains that he means that believing the mortal mind is death (sickness, trouble, limitations also belong to this), but when we only listen to the Spirit and not to the limited thoughts of the mortal mind, we truly live. The limited mind is like a shadow that the light of the Divine Mind throws in us. What it shows us is like the negative of a picture. Our so-called objective reality is an illusion. It is changeable. That which is real, is unchangeable. All the divine good is eternal. All the human good and evil is changeable and therefore not real. We certainly would not want to make it eternal.

9

The Thoughts of God.

Y ou don't have to have seen light or lightning flashes to recognize the Truth. You just know, you are absolutely certain. Others you tell about this, are also touched by it. They realize that it is irrefutable Truth. What our inner teacher, Divine Inspiration, tells us is absolutely true, for It does not reason, but knows. What the human intellect concludes could be true, but it is based on speculations. Even though divine Truth is unquestionable, at the same time you realize there is always more and you open your mind for revelations. Then you also learn to use your spiritual senses again and to perceive the divine light with it and the divine sound. You then live in the experience of oneness. You are only here to share the divine thoughts to which you have gained access. You cannot do anything else but give the divine understanding and the love that flows through you. You always teach, you teach what you are and what your convictions are. In this way you attract those who are in agreement with·your thought system and who want to share in it.

The right course of action is revealed to you under all circumstances. You are a channel for divine love and healing and miracles. Now you see that there are no limits to what we can experience. We are infinite and unlimited. You are happy and relieved now that you realize how insignificant your illusions about this form and our actions were. Through this realization you can forgive the world.

In our practice of the divine power in our lives we can have various experiences that do not belong to the normal human perception. We see light, hear unearthly sounds and perceive all sort of phenomena.

This makes us thankful. But the temptation here is to cling to the experiences and like an addict, want to see the same thing repeatedly. These phenomena are not our ultimate goal. We have to go on, further and further, to get to know the infinite divine reality. Many have perceived the less dense astral world and thought they were now 'enlightened'. Every experience that expands our consciousness should be welcomed. However, we should remember there is always more. Let us be aware of the temptation to use it to make up new limitations. For if we do so, we end up in excesses, like a so-called teacher of God with bodyguards, some even with weapons! Insanity reigns.

Belief and exploration belong together: every scientific investigation is based on chosen hypotheses, things one believes in and tries to prove. Since Divine Reality can only be proven in one's own experience, the existence of this will first have to be accepted by those to whom it has not been revealed through divine mercy. If this belief is followed by perceptual phenomena, like angels and gods, one will have to realize that the world of God is a spiritual world and therefore formless. Every form is still in the range of human perception. We are aware that experiences are also a possible trap. Glimpses of reality can also be a way to sedate yourself. As Liberty remarked: A little injection from Heaven to enable you to return and crucify yourself again. It is not meant to be used to remain in limitation.

Miraculous powers can also form a temptation. There are people who have learned to do without material food. Since food in whatever form and the need for food are ideas in the mind, that is quite possible. The body can take excellent care of itself, without any interference from us. You can just stop eating. It is your mind that is hungry. What is it good for, though? For what purpose do you develop this ability? It could be like the development of the ability to walk on fire. Many have spent their whole human lifespan developing this ability. They changed the way mankind viewed walking on fire and now it has become a common ability. But if the thinking is not healed, it just attaches itself to something else again.

Not eating then serves to show how 'special' you are and to impress others. Trying to live without food can focus the attention on something other than the communication with God and can be another diversion. Here too it is appropriate to first seek the kingdom of God. It is right and inevitable to live in glad anticipation of the gifts and revelations of God. For the Almighty has great plans for us. Everything is possible and we shall also experience that. It will exceed our greatest expectations.

We cannot measure the spiritual power that is God, through our limited human conceptions. God is everything we choose to experience in Him. The human mind can hardly envision the vastness of the physical universe. Let alone the infinite and all-encompassing Divine Mind.

Another possible stumbling block on our path is the temptation to turn things and people on our path into idols. The human thinking looks for God outside of itself. It needs teachers and learning situations. It asks its own projections where salvation can be found. Asking questions of something outside of yourself is usually from the ego. If questions come up you could ask your inner teacher. He makes sure that the answer is made clear in many aspects, by directing your attention to representations outside of you and by inner investigation. It is my experience that Divine Inspiration uses His channels that are apparently outside of you for this and when you are ready for it, you can hear the Voice for God inwardly. Just as your own purified thoughts, not as some dramatic voice outside of you. There is nothing outside of you and when you no longer identify with the ego, the Holy Spirit speaks in you and through you.

We seek salvation outside of ourselves and think we know where it can be found. The heart asks for happiness, then the mind attaches its own conditions to it. Man thinks he knows what brings happiness and instead of leaving it up to God, he wants to determine from which things and circumstances happiness can be expected.

Everything we seek outside of us has to disappoint us. Everything we learn from teachers or from anything in this world can at most be an approach to Truth. Divine wisdom, Truth, is accessible through our inner Teacher for each of us. All our learning is unlearning and remembering. When we think that a process of learning is necessary to perfect ourselves, then we actually suppose that God created us imperfect. For only something that is imperfect has to learn and be perfected. If God has created us in His image and likeness and we are imperfect, then God must also be imperfect!

Jesus said (Matthew 23:8–12): 'But be not ye called Rabbi: for one is your Master, even Christ; and all ye are brethren. And call no man your father upon the earth: for one is your Father, which is in heaven. Neither be ye called masters: for one is your Master, even Christ. But he that is greatest among you shall be your servant. And whosoever shall exalt himself shall be abased; and he that shall humble himself shall be exalted.'

People who allow themselves to be called master (or any other religious title) may only have the purpose to demonstrate that they are master of their own life. But usually those to whom they are a roadsign have wrong expectations. There is always the danger that the roadsign is elevated to an idol. We have applied separation to keep ourselves outside of the light. We have declared those who have shown us the path to enlightenment holy and thus placed enlightenment out of our reach.

Isn't it better then to follow someone who is farther on the path? Everyone who is still here in a mortal body is engaged in purification of the thought world. Those who consider themselves as more advanced than others, are mistaken. In fact the murderer is just as far as someone who lives a devoted life. The experience of a pious life may look more pleasant, but we share every experience. And every experience you see, is your experience, for we are totally connected and there is no experience we do not all share. Some people who describe a near-death experience give an interesting metaphor for that. They describe that they relived their life after their 'death', but also through the perspective of everyone they had contacted in their physical existence. They could feel everything the other had felt in that interaction.

Now the ego would make of this: watch out, for if you die, you will be punished by feeling everything you have done to another. This argument does not hold, for there is no guilt and therefore no punishment.

There is an even better argument. Suppose someone who was a prostitute and feels after she dies what her clients have felt. Would this form of empathy have the purpose to relive the physical satisfaction of someone else? No, it is an evaluation process. We then have the opportunity to completely see all sides of the coin in the dual life behind us and the various ways the matters we have experienced have been worked out. In that state of mind we can also judge which experiences we want to keep; which brought everyone involved peace and love and happiness? We look at the other experiences with amazement and sometimes maybe some sadness, because we have let so many opportunities to experience happiness pass by. The prostitute would therefore not merely relive the sexual feelings of her clients, she would experience how inadequate the instant intimacy was for the seeker. We relive every moment in which we express divine love and peace on a deeper level in our association with others. Therefore also the moments in which others reflected that love and peace in her. And especially the moments in which the remembrance of our true Self surfaced a moment. That is the goal of the overview of life. To remember who you really are. You don't have to 'die' for that purpose. Transformation begins as soon as you indicate that you are ready for it.

We are all teachers for each other. Everyone can learn from another. We are all a channel for the Holy Spirit or for the ego. Whether we represent the voice of fear and limitation or the one of love, everyone offers each other the opportunity to extend love in innumerable ways. The lessons that are suitable for each individual are already always presented to us. All those we can help to find the way to God, find their way to us.

The true teacher is the Holy Spirit. Without the Holy Spirit nothing is possible. The Holy Spirit knows all conflicts and deeply rooted convictions in the consciousness of everyone and is the perfect teacher. Liberation does not come from a human teacher. A human teacher is merely an instrument. If he thinks he is teaching, he is a spokesman for the ego and doomed to fail.

Under guidance of the Holy Spirit the ego naturally surrenders. Man is only the channel, the instrument and the teaching is mainly meant for the one who utters it. That is sometimes forgotten. Some teachers of God think they have to teach others and that they are the one who can teach. Of course You are. But it is from your Whole Mind, not from the limited mortal thought world, that this teaching comes. It is just that mortal thought world that has to be taught, that learns to let go of limitations and to expand consciousness.

What the 'teacher' also needs to realize is that that limited thought world is collective as well as personal. All thoughts in it are shared and at the same time individuals also take possession of fragments of them. But the thought-system of it is fundamentally identical. It is fearful and limited. It sees guilt and attack everywhere. It feels the need for defense. It doesn't realize that divine love and protection and care are everywhere and continual. God is omnipresent. God is almighty. Your belief determines what you will experience. That which you focus your attention on you experience. The question is: What do you want to believe? What do you want to experience? Behold what you are experiencing, then you know what you believe.

Our love for our teachers can turn into attachment, for there is the temptation to idolize. My teacher Joshua said: 'You believed there was something outside of you, and that you were dependent on it. You made idols, even though it is all in you. Whatever you think the teacher is, you already have to be. There is nothing outside of you. Whatever you think the teacher has, you must have.

Whatever you think the teacher expresses, you must be expressing. How else could you recognize it? Whatever you think you are, you are much more than that. You can learn from someone else, but you don't escape by imitating the behavior of someone else. Because your way out is unique and especial for you. Therefore, do not model yourself to be like another. You will express yourself in your own individual way. That will be whatever you want. You are free and unlimited in your choices in this.'

When we are guided by the Holy Spirit salvation is not difficult. He is a teacher who knows exactly which lessons you need and what is best suited for your frame of reference at any given moment. Those who are led to situations in which you feel uneasy or insulted, while your wrong identification is exposed, should remember that that which feels attacked, is not real. You are learning and can let go of wrong ideas about yourself, exactly because you begin to notice them. Your true Self then steps forward. You are cleansed of your limiting fearful ideas. You are ready to continue when you no longer need your teacher's approval, because you already approve of everything and everyone and are in total communication.

The teacher is a mouthpiece of you. It is you speaking through his mouth. You are using him or her as a channel. And you make no mistakes. You use the teacher to enable yourself to look at the way the ego that needs approval operates and judges with respect to the degree of enlightenment of another. If you see him as a personality and make an idol of him or her, you will be confronted with the effects of your thoughts. Only your own thoughts can hurt you. You crucify yourself. It is not possible to attack and remain out of the firing range. Whatever the attacker represents, is your own attack, your fear of salvation, for what you fear most, is your salvation. Everyone holds a mirror up for you, in which you see yourself and nothing else. A teacher can provide a safe environment where everyone knows what you are going through. If you are a beginner on the path, it can be helpful to share your beliefs in a group with others. But God is not found as part of a collective effort.

In this dream I have encountered the possibility of various degrees of enlightenment. Like writers and teachers who lacked integrity. They didn't live according to their own teaching. They preached detachment but were not able to set the example. Of course it is not a 'mortal sin' if one is not (yet) able to do that. Some feel they are better than others. But that too can be part of the awakening.

There are also teachers who have a very low opinion of their students. One 'enlightened' teacher said: 'In all the years that I do this, I have never seen anyone change.' And another wrote: 'Only the dregs of society come to me. Over and over I have to get them of drugs.' What is mostly the case with teachers is the dual thinking, the belief in an evil power, an adversary. They then speak of: 'They don't want you to make it.' There are also books, that are considered holy, that are filled with fear of demons and other idols of the human mind.

In whose thought world do these students appear? Who sees this evil? That question does not seem to occur to them. It is like a large blind spot. They don't realize that the thing they condemn appears in front of them and that that role is played by a loving neighbor to help them heal their judgment and illusions. For that which they see in their neighbor is not real. One who calls himself an enlightened teacher should at least be willing to be healed. It looks more like the ego has taken over the 'spiritual growth'. And then (temporary) stagnation follows.

I am aware that these forms of 'enlightenment' are also in my thought world. And I am willing to change my mind. I am grateful to my brothers who are willing to play the role of 'enlightened master' and in this way show me all degrees of enlightenment I have made up. When I perceive something like this, I say: 'I also am that. I have made it up and therefore I am that too. It is a ridiculous, senseless thought. It is caused by a need for love. But why would I want to be placed on a pedestal and be worshipped, if I am love? I only want to give love. And therefore no one has to lie at my feet or take my word as a law. I am aware that I have made those 'holy' words up and have tried to give them the status of absolute truth.'

That is how some books look, three pages of nonsense and 1 line of Truth. Unfortunately this nonsense confirms the illusions and so strengthens our error.

But it is impossible to completely repress Truth. It is there, between all superstition and littleness and makes our soul tremble. 'I am one with all my brothers and with my true Self, God, in everlasting perfect holiness and love. I am God. I am consciousness, Life. I am all-powerful, I can do anything I want to do. I control space and time. I am all-knowing. Everything I want to know appears in my consciousness. I am omnipresent, present everywhere, for I am everything in everything. I am love. There is only wholeness, for I am whole and I am everything.'

The belief in teachers outside of us who appear inwardly as light beings is prevalent. It seems to be difficult to recognize that you are that. The light you see is you. Just as all the nonsense you see. What you see is you. What you see outside of the light, is the shadow of it. And that doesn't mean 'the evil side of it' (that was the way in which human perception understood the word shadow), but a distorted reflection, colored by misunderstanding.

In 'The Masters of the Far-East' that is beautifully described by Jesus:

'There are so many who claim to be God's children and that they have everything the Father possesses. They do have everything the Father possesses, but this claim does not become fact until they have the courage to take the next step and see themselves as God, one with everything that God is. Only then can they accomplish everything. When someone who still thinks human and limited, sees the Christ appearing, that more finely tuned personality radiates light. He, who projects the Christ, then has a higher and wider perspective. He sees his own finer body vibrate at a faster rate than his limited body, which he also continues to see. He thinks there are two bodies. He also thinks that the body which he sees outside of him

and separated from him, is the Christ of someone else. But this only seems to be so, because he does not believe he is that same Christ. Let him announce himself as the Christ and accept this as fact; in that moment the two bodies will become one and he has manifested the Christ. Then the Christ steps forward triumphantly.'

And on another page: *'I tell you that now, on this moment, you have the opportunity to pass from all external turbulence into the great peace and blessings of God and to clothe yourself in Gods light.* **Place the crown of Christ with deep humility on your head, for if you don't do it yourself, no one else can do it for you.'**

Many temptations arise to take us back to the consciousness we have grown out of. But we can no longer depend on material and human sources. Whatever the form of the temptation, recognize it for what it is and it will pass.

How would you feel if you realized, every time when you are confronted with everything that does not belong to divine reality: This is not real, everything is perfect, I need do nothing. I only have to let the thought be made whole. And in this realization that is already done. You don't have to change anything, you only have to realize Reality, live in the recognition of it. You then escape from the prison of your own mind. You were your own jailer.

In the Presence of God all our problems dissolve in gentle laughter. That is what the Holy Spirit does with our fantasies, It laughs about them and tells us who we really are. God is in us, we are quickened by God. God gives us life. And for God all things are possible. Let us remember to ask for a miracle when we see problems in our lives or in that of others. Say quickly:

'Lord, use me. Let me be a channel for miracles and healing and for all your blessings. Thank You God.'

The realization that we no longer want to use the power of God to remain in limitation, and no longer want to return to verify ourselves, makes us determined in our focus on God. When we no longer use the energy to maintain all sorts of unpleasant emotions, like fear, jealousy and anger, then this is released and you feel like never before. It is often a state of euphoria and usually peace, with a deep constant inner vibration. It is as if you can step into it any moment, in that blissful stream of peace. It feels as if you step out of the shadow into the sunlight of love. To someone who has experienced that, the shadow has become very painful. In this transformation you become more and more sensitive to every disturbance of your inner peace. Your emotional life has become incredibly intense. Your thought world is filled with light. New revelations keep coming to you, knowledge that is revealed to you accompanied by a deeply felt knowing, and it really feels as if light permeates you and clothes you in a warm glow.

When you experience joy without mixed feelings or thoughts, love without fear, happiness without external cause, huge thankfulness wells up in your heart. You feel blessed and begin to praise and thank God. You cannot do anything else.

10

Acknowledging the Divine Power and denying dualism.

You are in an impossible situation, a world of suffering, sin, sickness, pain and death. A world in which you can lose things and people you love. During your childhood you learn various defenses against the misfortunes of human existence, only to discover that it is impossible to defend yourself against everything. Doom always strikes, in every life. And that is called life. It is death. Fear is what death is. The mortal existence is what death is. A miserable temporary existence, filled with fearful actions, with destination…what? An existence which you spend in search of that which you think will make you happy, money, status, sex, control of another that passes for love, you name it. All these things merely succeed in sedating you temporarily. It is not possible that they bring lasting fulfillment. Why? Because they do not last. None of the things you chase here will make you truly happy. And you know that, though you constantly try not to think of it. There is even the thought in mortal mind that this is all there is, that this is life and that we don't have to expect more. The height of hopelessness!

Is there an alternative then? Is there the possibility of a life that is filled with love, peace, and joy without opposite? Is it possible to escape from the dualistic world, the world in which you can experience temporary love and hate, dissatisfaction and mortal peace? Is it possible to escape from a world of experiences where joy is something of the moment, and based on something outside of you?

We are meant to be happy. The need for happiness and fulfillment of our needs is innate. But we don't know what will make us happy. As soon as we have something we thought would make us happy, we immediately start searching for something new. Nothing in this world satisfies us and until we cease the useless search, we will chase everything we think will ease our pain. It is the pain of our soul, longing to express itself. Life is enjoyment and not suffering, as we have been told so often. Life is only suffering if we believe in suffering.

Some people who have learned psychology are aware of the value of 'enjoyment' and living in the here and now. They try real hard and earnest to achieve that. But often happiness remains fleeting. Even if that isn't so, fear of loss soon surfaces. The remedy for that cannot be found through psychological self-analysis, but through spiritual Self-analysis. The current form of investigation of the personality is useless, for it is in every respect a wrong identification. There is individuality, but the personality is a caricature of that. It is useless to analyze the personality in the usual way, for it is Truth we are searching. It is difficult to see that a psychological solution is senseless. We tend to think that the behavior of people is formed through childhood experiences. That is only true as long as we believe that. Even then we are confronted with an abundance of anomalies, contradicting facts, for reality trickles into our perception continually. One example are the 'miracles' so many experience. Miracles happen all the time. They are often unlike anything the human mind pictures, they do not attract unwanted attention through spectacular and dramatic spectacles. Faith in the power of God and in divine reality is used everywhere to heal the thinking of humans and therefore also their physical, financial and other lack.

Some who embark on a spiritual search, have already tried everything they thought would make them happy. And they received it, but it did not live up to their expectations. They began to wonder if that was everything.

Others seem to have arrived at a low point in their lives from which they cannot come out by themselves. They are at their wits end and then turn to God.

The purpose is not to describe in detail in which situations man finally begins to realize that there has to be more, a better way. Such a time comes for everyone. And that is the invitation to God. Even though we often do not notice it at the moment, that is the moment we embark on our journey home. At the same time it is a story we invent, for we have never left our home. We know very well what it is like to experience everything we create immediately, but we wanted to experience it in time. Everyone has a script of awakening. When we can no longer tolerate this fearful place in our mind, and have had enough, our inner return begins. That is the moment we tell ourselves and God that we don't know anymore how to proceed and completely leave whatever happens to us to Him. Anything you can't, God can and anything you think you can, God can do much better. In God there is the perfect solution for any problem you can think of. If you give God the chance to give that solution, you give yourself the chance to be who you really are.

But the first step is the acknowledgement: God is! The only thing we are certain of here, is that there is a higher power. We can make up the attributes of God and therefore those are our ideas and concepts. Divine Spirit exists beyond any doubt. That does not need to be verified, for to whom would that have to be proven? To the no-spirit, the denial of God?

We are here to reveal the secret of our divine origin, the attributes of our Creator. Only then our lives are meaningful. Divine perfection exists, even if mankind is not yet able to express it. But you are always the best you you can be, right now. Man is giving the best of himself. He is returning and does that as fast as possible. The whole world is awakening.

The last lines of the Lord's Prayer are revealing. Spoken in full awareness of their meaning, they have the power to make us conscious immediately of Gods might and omnipresence.

'For Thine is the kingdom
and the power and the glory,
For ever
Amen.'

Though this ending is not included in Lucas and it also does not appear in many of Matthew's writings, it is logical that the prayer should end with honoring and praising God, if it wells from our heart. Our inner being is then overflowing with gratitude for the magnitude of the divine gifts and we can do nothing else.

These last lines help us to realize that God is the only power. It is the acknowledgement of God as our Creator and the Source of everything. There is no good and evil, there is only God. With this we deny every dualism. This is effective denial. There is nothing that wants to punish us or limit us. Nothing but our own thoughts. Though negative experiences and circumstances appear to us, we have to deny that they are caused by God or another evil power. They are caused by our ignorance about the effect of our thoughts. We can see the divine present, by letting go of our acquired definitions based on our experiences. By letting go what we perceive with the eyes of the body, with the help of the Holy Spirit.

We are here exploring possibilities. None of us ever really left Heaven. This is just a mind game.

How do you know if this is really true, if they are not just delusions of grandeur?

Everything you think is true, is true for you. Your reality may seem firm, but the moment you start exploring the possibility that it is not so, that maybe you are a whole, holy being, the whole universe supports your endeavor. You will find that the Truth is supported from the inner knowledge, as opposed to deducting and believing what others have taught you.

And then your reality changes too. It is not just a matter of a change in interpretation; when you see the Christ in everyone, it is the Christ who comes forward to meet you.

How do you go about that, how do you explore?

There are many ways to do that. You have to work with a few basic principles in mind.

1. You cannot know your own reality, if you deny that of others. You cannot see the Christ in yourself, if you don't see It in others. Everybody is a mirror of your self-concept. Therefore, you practice forgiveness, or the undoing of your picture of people and circumstances. You don't do that by approving that which is obviously wrong, you do that by seeing that the other is not that. He is just slumming, exploring the slums in the mind, exploring a horrible idea and outpicturing his beliefs. And if you equate him with his role, they are also your beliefs. Let them become your old beliefs and they will go away. Let go of all thoughts of guilt and of right or wrong. There is only true or false. And in every circumstance, ask yourself, how God would view this. Ask yourself if God would do the things you are witnessing. It's called 'practicing the Presence' and it is a lot of fun. You will find yourself laughing a lot.

2. You start thinking and acting like the Being that you really are. You do everything in accordance with your true being. Never mind the appearance of mistakes. Gradually your old conditioning will fade away. 'Be you perfect, as your father in heaven is perfect' said Jesus. Ask Him in every situation what He would have you do and say, where He would have you go. Surrender to Yourself.

Your ego may not like it, but your ego does not like anything that is good for you.

You have given attributes to everything you perceive, everything in your experience. Let go of your definition of yourself and of the other and accept a new definition. Let go of all your definitions and interpretations. You, Adam, human, were allowed to name everything, and this is the way you have done that. When you let go of your definitions, things can testify of their perfection.

Let us accept the Truth, that God is Love and that it is the Will of God, that we are happy. When we trust in the power of God, that makes all the difference in our lives. There is only the power of God and outside of His kingdom nothing is real. The kingdom of God is in our consciousness, it is our own mind. What God has not made, is not known, for God does not know it. In infinite Mind all thoughts are and therefore also the thought what a world without God would look like. This impossible possibility is viewed by us and when we have enough of our foolish child's game, we will return to the kingdom, that is ours. We then are conscious co-creators with God and channels for divine manifestation. First we do have to know the rules of the game. You can only participate effectively if you learn to bring consciously into your experience that which reality reflects.

We will take back our power and restore the communication with our Source. Then we have found the priceless pearl, the life of God-realization and knowledge of divine Truth. In timelessness we already have. For this world we think we are perceiving, is over and gone a long time ago. We are merely looking at the past. In the timeless eternity only the Divine Spirit is real. And that we affirm and we say: Amen, so it is.

0-595-24839-X